CRYPTO ECONOMY

CRYPTO ECONOMY

*How Blockchain, Cryptocurrency,
and Token-Economy Are Disrupting
the Financial World*

ARIES WANLIN WANG

CO-FOUNDER OF BIBOX DIGITAL ASSET EXCHANGE

FOREWORD BY KEVIN BARRY

CEO, MYNTUM LIMITED
PRESIDENT, FIRST FREEDOMS, INC.

Racehorse Publishing

Racehorse Publishing books may be purchased in bulk at special discounts for sales promotion, corporate gifts, fund-raising, or educational purposes. Special editions can also be created to specifications. For details, contact the Special Sales Department, Skyhorse Publishing, 307 West 36th Street, 11th Floor, New York, NY 10018 or info@skyhorsepublishing.com.

Racehorse Publishing™ is a pending trademark of Skyhorse Publishing, Inc.®, a Delaware corporation.

Visit our website at www.skyhorsepublishing.com.

10 9 8 7 6 5 4 3 2 1

Library of Congress Cataloging-in-Publication Data is available on file.

Cover design by Kaili Zhang

ISBN: 9781-5107-4482-0
Ebook ISBN: 9781-5107-4483-7

Printed in the United States of America

CONTENTS

Foreword by Kevin Barry, CEO of Myntum Limited   *vii*

Chapter 1: How Does Something like Bitcoin Happen?   1

Chapter 2: Blockchain Evolving—From 1.0 to 2.0   19

Chapter 3: Gold Rush—Today's Mining Opportunity   31

Chapter 4: Vocean—Decentralizing Financial Services   47

Chapter 5: The Top of the Food Chain and the Birth of Crypto Exchanges   59

Chapter 6: The Secondary Market: Low-Lying Land   71

Chapter 7: Beyond Boundaries—Crypto Economics around the World   83

Chapter 8: Getting Along with Regulators   97

Chapter 9: Blockchain—Assets Protector   105

Chapter 10: The Future of Blockchain   113

Glossary of Terms   *119*

FOREWORD
by Kevin Barry, CEO of Myntum Limited

"Nothing is more powerful than an idea whose time has come."
—Victor Hugo

We are at a turning point in worldwide financial transactions. Who will embrace change and who will be left behind? Decentralization, trust, privacy, and democratization of financial transactions are all ideas whose time has come. Blockchain technology will certainly drive these ideas over the next few years; the question is: Where will this happen? Some governments will embrace the technology of the future and others will resist, steadfastly clinging to the status quo. Who wins and who loses?

In *Crypto Economy: How Cryptocurrency, Blockchain, and Token Economy Are Disrupting the Financial World*, Aries Wanlin Wang expertly describes how this revolutionary new economy will function. As an insider who cofounded exchanges and has functioned successfully in the crypto economy over many years, he is the ultimate guide to this sometimes confusing new economy. Readers will no doubt benefit from his perspective and understanding of the concerns and motives of the people who make the economy work.

Through my varied professional experiences, I have insight into the concerns and motivations of various nations and regulators to this new technology. As a representative of a Nongovernmental Organization (NGO) at the United Nations in New York City, I have heard the concerns of technology and information ministers from multiple countries all around the world. I am formerly an attorney for the United States government, so I have insight into how government regulators react when faced with new technologies. I am also the CEO of a startup company called Myntum Limited, which is building online vaults to secure critical digital assets (including cryptocurrencies and tokens). For this reason, I have been closely following developments in the crypto economy for the past two years. Finally, I am the founder of a nonprofit organization called First Freedoms, which advances the five freedoms listed in the First Amendment to the United States Constitution (freedoms of religion, speech, press, assembly, and redress of grievances). What is the link between the First Amendment and crypto economy?

Both have their foundation in freedom. In the late 18th century, the ideas and ideals of the First Amendment became part of the bedrock of the US's emphasis on individual freedom. Now is the time for the ideas and ideals of blockchain and the crypto economy. And yet there are still questions that remain, which must ultimately be addressed:

- Decentralization or centralization?
- Trust between parties or a Third Party to ensure trust?
- Transparency of transactions or hidden and opaque transactions?
- A borderless world with less political influence or a bordered world with more political influence?
- Crowdfunding for new businesses or only venture capital, investment banks, and governments?

These are only a few of the ideas citizens, businesses, and government regulators will have to sort out.

How do governments make decisions on new technology? In general, governments have three options: support, oppose, or no position. The crypto economy desires support or neutral positions from governments. To accomplish this, most people in the crypto economy know they need to work with governments in various jurisdictions to enact smart regulation to help make the new economy thrive. Working with friendly jurisdictions to make the new crypto economy thrive also allows for the possibility of convincing governments that oppose it to change their policy.

So, decentralization or centralization? For centuries, financial transactions have required centralized banks or financiers—national banks, commercial banks, credit card issuers—to act as "trusted Third Parties" to facilitated transactions between two parties. Until blockchain technology arrived in 2008, no one had developed a sound and safe way to bypass the banks. With blockchain technology, individuals and businesses for the first time have the power to deal directly with each other. This sounds ideal, but there are important issues to work out, and I believe that sometimes involving a trusted Third Party is a good choice.

Trust between parties or requiring a Third Party to ensure trust? The crypto economy provides individuals and businesses the option to either deal directly with each other or to deal in the traditional "fiat" currency economy involving a Third Party. I believe the future of cryptocurrency acceptance will involve crypto being used for relatively small purchases and fiat currency being used for relatively large purposes. At this time, there is no good method of dispute resolution in the cryptocurrency markets. There is no crying in crypto. If a transition goes badly, there is no one to complain to. In which jurisdiction would you file a complaint? I believe in the near future those involved in large transactions will continue use the traditional economy, but this is still good news for crypto! Most of the routine transactions every day are small transactions that are perfect for cryptocurrencies.

Transparency of transactions or hidden or opaque transactions? Cryptocurrency transactions are transparent on a public ledger for the world to see. Each Bitcoin can only be used once. This is a radical departure from the fiat traditional economy, which uses the same dollar multiple times. The brilliant Ray Dalio of Bridgewater Associates described this in 2014 in "How the Economic Machine Works":

> Virtually all of what the Federal Reserve calls money is credit (i.e., promises to deliver money) rather than money itself. The total amount of debt in the US is about $50 trillion and the total amount of money (i.e., currency and reserves) in existence is about $3 trillion. So, if we were to use these numbers as a guide, the amount of promises to deliver money (i.e., debt) is roughly 15 times the amount of money there is to deliver.

As long as the gears of this economic machine are turning, the music is playing and there is no one scrambling for a seat in musical chairs. But if and when the music stops, there are fifty people fighting over three seats. This is what happens in economic crises. Because each Bitcoin can only be used once, this type of problem cannot happen.

A borderless world with less political influence or a bordered world with more political influence? I'm an idealist. I am very much drawn to the idea of a borderless world. Technology is borderless. Financial transactions in theory can be borderless. In the traditional fiat economy and in the crypto economy, assets can be sent anywhere at the click of a mouse. This is not the reality, however. Governments sometimes get into disagreements and sanction one another and prohibit their citizens from doing business with one another. Businesses and individuals should absolutely respect the sanctions that their countries impose. A simple business principle? Respect and honor any regulator who can close you, litigate and fine you out of existence, or put you in prison.

Cryptocurrencies are a borderless world with less political influence. Algorithms don't get into ego-driven damaging political contests with one another. Algorithms don't get into trade wars, or exchange tariffs. Algorithms don't have historic rivalries, military ambitions, or leaders in search of glory. The borderless world and cryptocurrencies have great potential to democratize economic transactions and economic opportunity to the benefit of individuals all over the world.

Crowdfunding for new businesses or only venture capital, investment banks, and governments? Initial coin offerings, now more commonly called Token Generating Events (TGE), are simply crowdfunding. I believe that this democratization of business fundraising holds great promise, with smart regulation. Governments have a legitimate interest in stopping frauds. This is true in both the traditional economy and the crypto economy.

Regulations on TGEs vary greatly country by country. G20 countries with the largest economies are generally wary of upsetting the status quo. Their current economic policies have them in the G20! Many of the 180 countries NOT in the G20 are willing to experiment. The top twenty economies in the world hold 80 percent of the world's wealth. The other 172 countries are less thrilled with the status quo and view the crypto economy differently. This is a frequent topic of conversation at the United Nations. The developing world views the crypto economy and blockchain technology as a potential way to improve the lives of their citizens through TGEs.

Crypto economy and blockchain leaders need to work with regulators to realize the potential of the technology. It's important to understand that countries take their currencies seriously. Government planners in the United States, China, and the European Union are concerned about the potential of capital flight. Economists in the G20 countries might have to make projections based on imperfect data if they can't figure out how to track every transaction!

The elephant in the room regarding governments is taxes. The crypto economy will need to work with governments regarding taxation as the markets mature. This cooperation will be a complicated culture clash, but I think it is necessary and will benefit all parties in the long term. Countries don't want to push their best and brightest citizens, the businesses they will start, and the jobs they will create over borders.

The First Amendment of the United States Constitution empowered individual freedoms and helped remake the contract between citizens and governments over 200 years ago. I believe the crypto economy and blockchain technology can empower economic freedom for individuals and rewrite the way the globe does business.

Read on, and Aries Wanlin Wang will explain how.

—Kevin Barry, September 2018

1.

HOW DOES SOMETHING LIKE BITCOIN HAPPEN?

In late 2008, under the long shadow cast by the most severe economic crisis in generations, a revolutionary new form of currency was quietly being shaped. Initially, there was no clue that an obscure form of electronic money would prove to be the most important financial innovation of the 21st century, a tool that would soon be widely adopted by people, economies, and companies all across the world. In October of that year, in a white paper issued by an anonymous person or group calling itself Satoshi Nakamoto—now known to the world as "the creator of Bitcoin"—the digital currency known as Bitcoin, and the technologies underpinning it, were laid out for the first time. There were few clues in this initial description that made anyone think Bitcoin had the power to upend and revolutionize the world's financial system. Bitcoin's success was far from assured.

In its early days, Bitcoin was mostly seen as an oddity—something that was only around to amuse experts in cryptography. Just ten years ago, the general public was still mostly unfamiliar with cryptocurrency. It was only for specialists and eccentrics. Today, of course, Bitcoin has become a household name. It has the highest market value of any cryptocurrency. Moreover, it has drawn an enormous amount of attention to blockchain, the technology on which it is built. (If you've ever been to a blockchain conference, you will truly feel the "electricity in the air" of the great expectations people now hold for the future of blockchain technology. Bitcoin has had its ups and downs, but this enthusiasm has not abated.) Blockchain was originally developed as a sort of "storage room" for Bitcoin—something that would record transactions and avoid the possibility of the currency being used inappropriately. The focus of this book will be the technical backbone of cryptocurrency and the crypto economies it makes possible. But before we get into the thick of it, we need to spend a moment on Bitcoin and its history, because Bitcoin was the driver of it all. It's just that important.

The disaster of the subprime mortgage crisis in 2008 shook the public's confidence in banks, governments, and other powerful institutions. Suddenly, everything was in doubt. Entities that had been seen as rock-solid and trustworthy for generations appeared to have abruptly let us down. They had been revealed as empty facades. The emperors had no clothes. Now, the world was looking for new solutions. And into this environment, Bitcoin arrived like a magic bullet, seemingly designed to solve the very issues that had caused the financial crisis in the first place. Bitcoin would decentralize power. There would be no external arbiter or regulator that might fail us. To the contrary, the people—the users of the cryptocurrency themselves—would truly hold the power.

But perhaps Bitcoin was not only successful because it arrived on the scene at just the right time. One must admit that it also has a sense of mystery about it, an allure that many found romantic and daring. Bitcoin was exclusive at first, like a club that people wanted to join. It was initially introduced to a very small group of people—experts in cryptography and "tech nerds" who were obsessed with the concept of individual liberty. (Some called these people "cypherpunks.") Just as one sees in the trajectory of any exclusive brand, Bitcoin gradually made itself more available to the masses. Yet even as consumers scrambled to get in on the hip, new "Bitcoin rush," many did not truly understand what the currency was, and the transformative power it held. But for us to discuss that here, we need to take a brief look at the history of money.

Sumer is an ancient civilization that was founded in Mesopotamia around the year 3000 BC. Sumerians are generally understood to be the first people who used money as a medium to facilitate exchange. Before the Sumerians, humans mostly used a barter system to make exchanges—trading things for other physical things. There are many disadvantages to a barter system.

For example, say it's winter, and you'd like some wood to heat your house. You raise sheep and cows. Your neighbor grows trees, and he would like to have some meat for his family. You and your neighbor have to work out a barter arrangement—say, one sheep for twenty wood blocks. You give him your sheep, and he gives you his blocks. Sure, it works, but it's not as easy as using money.

The direct exchange of goods without a universally accepted medium brings all kinds of inefficiencies and issues. If you don't have anything your neighbor wants, for example, then a trade cannot happen. As a way around these issues, we invented money and credit, which remain the foundations of our economy today. Today, if you want wood blocks, you can use credit or debt to borrow twenty wood blocks from your neighbor—which puts you in his debt but allows you to pay him in the future. You can also simply pay him for the wood blocks in cash, which he can then spend any way he likes. Either works if your neighbor trusts you and/or trusts the currency you give him. Credit and money enable trade and make it more efficient.

And now, after 3000 years of financial and technological evolution, the Internet has brought us to a digital version of ancient Sumer. Since the Internet was first invented in 1969, half a century has gone by. In the intervening time, the Internet has become an inextricable part of our lives. Many of us can live without our girlfriends or boyfriends, but not without access to the Internet! The Internet connects people wirelessly and instantly through emails, social media, online businesses, and more. The extent of the social and financial engagements we are forging through the Internet reveal just how much we rely on it in every aspect of our lives.

The benefits of the Internet are clear. But there are also downsides. Some of the biggest downsides that we really can't ignore involve privacy and security. Namely, how can we protect our privacy and stay safe when all of our photos and personal information are all over the web?

For most of us, the answer has been to allow centralized, trusted authorities to verify and safely enable activities conducted online. In a way, it's similar to how we've decided to let governments and banks oversee, manage, and control our economic transactions. Companies like Facebook, Google, Microsoft, and IBM have all—in different ways—become part of the apparatus we trust to provide safety online. The information we use is stored in central servers owned by powerful Internet companies. These companies provide services we value, and in return we trust them with our personal information. Yet once our information is in their hands, we have very little control over how they may use or exploit it. Think of how frequently we learn that a web company has been selling user information without permission. Think of how frequently websites change their terms of service, allowing customer data to be sold or used in other ways. Facebook's recent scandal is an excellent example of the violations of privacy and abuses of power that many users feel are unfairly foisted on them month after month.

Yet no matter how one feels about the Internet, it's undeniably *the* major force pushing us into the future. Much like banks, Internet-based giants have become too big to fail. Google dominates information exchange through the prevalence of its search engine. Dominant social media platforms such as Facebook control personal connections and public information exchange. E-commerce has also become a part of our lives, with Amazon and Alibaba the unshakable giants in the field.

Theft of personal information is one thing, but the potential for the theft of online financial information presents a whole new ball game. For many people across the world, the ritual of going to the bank in person has been replaced by completing our financial transactions online. As the hard times in retail evince, we also now buy and sell merchandise online with increasing frequency. And instead of picking up the phone and calling restaurants to place our orders, we now browse menus and make orders on the web. This increase in online financial activity demands better security and efficiency. Cryptocurrency was created for this. It provides better security and is easier to use. We don't need to reveal our identities when we make purchases using cryptocurrencies. And that fact, vitally, means we can choose to remain anonymous.

CYPHERPUNKS, LIBERTARIANISM, AND DIGITAL MONEY

It took the public a while to migrate from digital money (transferring digital dollars online) to using cryptocurrency—that is, money created using cryptography. But that migration *is* now happening. Yet to truly understand a phenomenon like this, we need to ask *why* it is happening. Why did people want to create a currency separate from the fiat money controlled by the central governments and central banks?

Diners Club is generally considered to have been the birth of the credit card. In 1974, Roland Moreno invented the IC card as a medium to store digital currency. In 1982, the United States created the electronic funds transfer system (EFTS), with Great Britain and Germany creating similar institutions shortly thereafter. Credit cards issued by banks were an instant hit, expanding exponentially as demand increased. This was the first digitizing of fiat money. It was important because it changed our perception of money in a way it hadn't been in centuries. For the first time, most of us didn't need to carry cash around. Everything could be done virtually.

Even though digital money is very different from—and exists in a different form from—fiat money, it still relies on the centralized oversight of powerful banks and governments. Not everybody likes this because of the inherent requirements and regulations. Namely, unlike cash, you can't use your credit card anonymously. You're charged a special rate to use your credit card in another country.

Some cards are not accepted at all in certain countries. And middlemen—such as banks and finance companies—play major roles in the transactions. PayPal and Ali Pay likewise present themselves as "trusted third-party payment options," yet their presence removes our ability to make many transactions discreetly or anonymously. International money transactions from one bank to another are also impossible without going on the public record.

To better capture customer and seller information, online middlemen have also attempted to introduce invasive technologies like Public Key that require both buyer and seller to go through complicated processes to verify their identities whenever they make a transaction. However, the birth of Bitcoin has largely derailed the adoption of these new systems.

The ability to make anonymous payments and transactions online has always had the support of certain communities, such as IT elites, cryptographers (the so-called cypherpunks), advocates of decentralization, and people on the libertarian side of the political spectrum. There is something of a communal identity involved—some shared worldview between these groups. They feel part of a fraternity influenced by thinkers like Friedrich August von Hayek. When barriers to free commerce like Public Key appeared on the horizon, cypherpunks and their kin aimed to create a new way of exchanging information (financial and otherwise) that would have little or no interference from the new regulators. They wanted to enhance privacy and protect personal freedom. They also wanted to actively subvert the government and its attempts at regulation.

All of these desires seemed to actualize themselves in Bitcoin.

Back in the 1980s, Timothy May proposed an idea for digital money that he called "Crypto Credits." David Chaum was the first to apply cryptography to E-cash. Yet one of the major issues that E-cash faced was called "Double Spend." This, more or less, is what it sounds like. Money is spent twice. Transactions are redeemed twice. It's like taking a check to one bank and cashing it, and then being able to take it to another bank and cash it again. For example, say that the User A issues $1 in E-cash through an E-signature to User B. The risk is that User B will then duplicate User A's E-signature to get two dollars instead of one.

An early solution calculated to solve the Double Spend problem was printing a unique serial number on each note issued. When the note was sent out from User A, User B would check the signature and make a phone call to User A, asking him or her for the serial number, and if the E-cash note had been used previously. If the note had *not* been cashed before, User B would accept the note. User A would then document that the note had been used.

Whew. Is it any wonder that a system like this did not catch on?

In today's the digital world, servers complete all the work, including documenting every signature and serial number involved in financial transaction. Using serial numbers solved the Double Spend problem, but it did not allow individuals to transact anonymously, since each transaction (and corresponding personal information) could be tracked through the serial number.

To try and make each transaction anonymous, David Chaum then proposed a work-around known as "Blind Signature," which basically solves two problems at once—anonymity and double spend. It allows the user to perform any monetary exchange that actual, physical money would allow (except perhaps physically flipping coins). How does Blind Signature work? It all takes place in an "envelope." User A puts a note with a serial number into the "envelope," which no one has access to except for User A. But then how does User B sign the note without his or her identity becoming known? The answer is to insert a carbon paper into the "envelope"—the signature will then appear on the note through the carbon paper. However, User B doesn't know the serial number, and User A doesn't know who signed the note.

The bottom line is that a transaction will take place with two parties not knowing each other's identity.

Using this technology, David Chaum started two companies. One, DigiCash, was created to provide digital payments online using E-cash. The other, Cyberbucks, was designed to provide support for banks.

E-cash was a very refreshing solution, but like a cool drink enjoyed too quickly, the refreshment it provided lasted only for a few moments! Despite its advantages, it was never able to get mainstream acceptance. Even though it was designed to help buyers and sellers facilitate transactions, few sellers saw a benefit in using it.

It's a different story when it comes to Bitcoin—and we'll discuss those differences later in this book. But regardless of the failure to commercialize its E-cash service, the concept of Blind Signature was a vital and important milestone in the history of digital currency.

David Chaum applied for patents for the technologies related to E-cash, including Blind Signature, a move that received some criticism as hindering the advancement of e-payments. However, this did not stop cypherpunks, who continued using Blind Signature to develop better payment solutions. Ten years after DigiCash went into bankruptcy, Satoshi revealed the birth of Bitcoin to the world. And most of the people on Satoshi's email list were these very cypherpunks.

Let's spend a little more time thinking about these cypherpunks, and what exactly they wanted to accomplish. Julian Assange might be a good example of a "distinguished cypherpunk," but he's not the only one. Cypherpunks share a passion for individual liberty. Assange was clearly passionate about making information available and accessible to the public. Cypherpunks feel the same way about cryptocurrency. They believe private financial transactions should be available to the public, decentralizing the existing banking system, avoiding inflation, and improving security. Cypherpunks also seek to avoid the calamities that have hit the world economy in recent years. The crisis of 2008 shook global confidence in the ability of governments and major financial institutions to effectively control the economy. To cypherpunks, Bitcoin presented a new hope by proposing a solution that would allow users to avoid the mistakes of the past entirely.

But despite the fondest wishes of the cypherpunk crowd back in 2008, Bitcoin and other cryptocurrencies have yet to be accepted as widely as fiat money. Yet, at the same time, Bitcoin has generated tremendous global awareness through its disruptive spirit and its astronomical increase in value. Because its benefits are so clear, and it is so appealing to so many people, many governments are actively trying to establish ways to work with it.

Next, I'd like us to consider cryptocurrency against regular currencies by looking at how currencies are issued.

THE EVOLUTION OF CRYPTOGRAPHY

For hundreds of years, central banks have been playing one of the most critical roles in the financial system by managing how much money is released into the market, and controlling when this release happens. This is true for fiat money, and also for traditional digital money. In order to be accepted as a legitimate currency, digital money needs to represent value and be able to carry value. As I mentioned earlier, digital money is merely another form of fiat money. It is, essentially, the same thing. It relies on a trusted third party to verify every transaction. Cryptocurrency, however, has no need for a third party. Another way to put this is that it cuts out the middleman. Cryptocurrencies are also different from fiat money in that they are backed up by cryptography. Cryptography has two critical functions, encryption and verification, which are accomplished through coding and decoding.

Cryptography as a science was widely applied during World War II. Fighting alongside the soldiers of the the allied armies were mathematicians and engineers who used cryptography to wage a silent war of information. As the Germans used their famous Enigma machine to transfer coded orders, allied cryptographers fought against time to decipher it.

Today, cryptography is widely applied in a variety of economic functions and situations. Cryptography has become especially useful in computer science, and notably in the area of Internet security. With every single browser click, we interact with pages running on a complicated system of codes. Cryptography secures the input and output of information on these pages.

In the 1970s, the field of cryptography saw major innovations. Whitfield Diffie and Marty Hellman invented the so-called "Diffie and Hellman Key Exchange" in 1976, which enabled modern e-commerce and encrypted communication. In 1977, Ron Rivest, Adi Shamir, and Leonard Adelman came up with the RSA—a powerful encryption engine of great commercial value. And in 1985, Neal Koblit and Victor Miller introduced ECC—an approach to public-key cryptography based on the algebraic structure of elliptic curves over finite fields.

Encryption is the backbone of Internet security, telecommunication, and also of cryptocurrencies like Bitcoin. In their earliest stages, the government had absolute control over encryption algorithms. The NSA kept a close eye on who was using them. It was only in the 1990s that these algorithms were released to the public. Interestingly enough, the NSA is known to have planted backdoor entryways into the technologies released to the public to enable the NSA weaken or disorient certain content at will.

Bitcoin is lucky enough to have avoided the backdoor "way in" planted by the NSA. Satoshi Nakamoto, the father of Bitcoin, went with an algorithm that was not popular enough to be on the NSA's radar. As confirmed by no less than Vitalik Buterin, the founder of Ethereum, Satoshi made many lucky decisions when crafting his creation, and among them was choosing the right algorithm to avoid the traps planted by the NSA. There are only few programs existing today that have been able to successfully avoid the NSA loophole. The sense of security this gives users may be yet another reason for Bitcoin's success.

Bitcoin is the best example of the value of blockchain technology. In Satoshi's white paper from 2008, it's made clear that blockchain will be the backbone of the exchange system for Bitcoin users. It will be, as Satoshi puts it, "a purely peer-to-peer version of electronic cash [allowing] online payments to be sent directly from one party to another without going through a financial institution." Using cryptographic technology to secure payment has eliminated the need for banks—or other institutions—to act as middlemen.

SO HOW DOES IT WORK WITH BITCOIN?

A person making transactions with Bitcoin uses an electronic wallet, which has an IP address containing that person's public "key" and other identification. It is this wallet that allows the person to send and receive Bitcoins, and to document each transaction. Beside the public key, the Bitcoin user also has her or his own private key to which only they have access. This double encryption helps users of Bitcoin to remain anonymous. In order to verify a Bitcoin transaction, users have to contribute computer power to the blockchain to achieve a consensus. Transactions are then documented into blocks spread across the entire chain. One way to think of this is that blockchain allows a permanent record to be kept of each Bitcoin transaction and eliminates the possibility of so-called double payments. Blockchain is essential to Bitcoin and is what allows for the cryptocurrency's decentralization and disintermediation. Each block in the chain nests information that cannot be altered. Trust is created by the technology itself and the way it provides total transparency.

But how exactly does blockchain prevent people from cheating or committing fraud? It's a fair question.

I don't want to get too technical here, but cryptography is the key. In the chain of blocks that is the blockchain, every block has something called a Hash Pointer, which points to and reveals the Hash Value contained in the block in the front of the chain. With this Hash Pointer in place, it is impossible to hack the blockchain. Once a block is created and accepted, it is almost impossible to alter. At a primordial, technical level, this means the blocks and the transactions they record are virtually inalterable.

We've already discussed some of the issues involved in preserving anonymity when conducting transactions with digital money. Any truly anonymous transaction involves a public key and a private key. However, it also involves a digital signature and asymmetric cryptography, which we should also examine.

The terms might sound complicated, but the concept is not hard to explain. Asymmetric cryptography gives every user two keys, a public key and a private key. The public key presents the identification and the IP address of the account holder. It can also encrypt information. Whatever information the public key encrypts can only be decoded by the matching private key. If a user is using a private key to sign any information, only the matching public key can verify the authenticity of the signature. In this world of decentralization, there is no need for a centralized power—like a bank, or software company, or government entity—to manage or secure any user's information. Users open their accounts and keep their private key. Bitcoin users (and users of any other cryptocurrencies) often use the word *address* to refer to the Hash Value of the public key. The private key stays in the control of each user. In this way, asymmetric cryptography cuts out the government and any other entities who, in the physical world, collect and manage our identification information to verify transactions.

Peer-to-peer network technology was the final element that had to fall into place to ensure the birth of Bitcoin. When most people think of this kind of technology, they think of something like Napster.

Napster, founded by Sean Fanning and Shawn Parker in 1999, was the first music application that allowed people to share music from one computer to another, directly over the Internet. Due to copyright problems and lawsuits, Napster ceased to exist in the first year of the 21st century. Yet despite its ultimate failure, it was important because it proved that peer-to-peer technology works, and that it can be adopted and deployed on a massive scale.

THE BIRTH OF BITCOIN

The nine-page white paper released by Satoshi Nakamoto in October of 2008 starts with the words "A purely peer-to-peer version of electronic cash would allow online payments to be sent directly from one party to another without going through a financial institution." With these words, Satoshi was throwing down the gauntlet. He had identified the problem and also proposed the solution. Bitcoin would be different from other digital money because it would be detached from centralized power.

For his project to work, Satoshi would have to get the world comfortable with the idea of decentralized power. It sounds daunting, but is it really such a radical shift? We experience decentralization in our daily lives each day. We use email all the time, for example, and the Simple Mail Transfer Protocol is a decentralizing system.

But in order to accomplish his goal of promulgating a system based on decentralization, Satoshi knew he would also have to solve the issue of distributed consensus.

What exactly is distributed consensus? The story of the Byzantine Generals has often been used to help explain the concept.

The story goes like this: Byzantium was once the most powerful empire in the world, but it was also very big, extending throughout Europe and Asia. The territory under its control was bigger than the United States. Whenever there was a war, armies were dispatched away from the central government. Each army was led by one general operating independently. The problem was how to ensure that the generals would stay loyal out in the field, and how to detect if a general had become a traitor. Things came to a head when generals were called upon to either make a coordinated attack or make a coordinated retreat. (The consequences of half of the generals doing one, and half the other, would be calamitous.) When the generals communicated with one another—and one heard from another that an attack or retreat was called for—how would each general know he was not dealing with a traitor?

Cryptographers encountered the same problem. Namely, how to reach an agreement when there are many "generals" spreading out peer-to-peer information in the blockchain? Satoshi solved the problem of distributed consensus through something called Proof of Work. Simply put, honest work gets rewards.

Proof of Work was first tested by Adam Back, a British cryptographer, who in 1996 developed a software for fighting off junk emails. The system he designed required every received email to be sent with certain proof of how much time and effort had been put into creating the email. This gave spammers trying to send junk email a headache because they had to put work into meeting the standard in order for their emails to pass the test and land in the targeted recipient's email box. But since not many people used email back in 1996 (at least not compared to now), the issue of junk spam email didn't get the attention it gets today. Consequently, Back's system did not get a chance to be widely adopted. However, the innovation that his software had created would go on to be very useful in the future.

From an economical point of view, Proof of Work increases the cost of inputting false information. To release a block into the chain of a blockchain takes a considerable amount of computer power. Being the first one to release a block into the system can be very time- and energy-intensive. When you hear about miners "mining Bitcoins," they are actually creating new blocks or verifying new transactions in the chain. The Bitcoin blockchain accordingly rewards these miners through Proof of Work for their efforts.

If 10,000 hours make a person an expert in a certain field—as the adage goes—then it is the same in the world of Bitcoin, where miners have to prove their work through Hash Function. In addition to being a long process, it's also a very complicated process. Miners need to solve all kinds of mathematical problems. The result of successfully solving those problems is receiving Bitcoins. Whenever a new block in a blockchain is created, the miner will be rewarded with a certain amount of Bitcoins. And when a new piece of transaction is put into blocks, then the miner will be rewarded with a certain amount of Bitcoins depending on who initiated the transaction.

Proof of Work runs in a space where there is no need for "trust" in the traditional sense, because everything is verified by the system. As long as you get your work done, you will be rewarded. It's almost impossible to cheat in this process. There are many types of cryptocurrencies currently using Proof of Work to validate transactions and create new blocks, including Bitcoin, Litecoin, Dogecoin, and Monero.

The more blocks in a chain, the more information released into blocks will make the system more solid and safer, yet at the same time, more energy will be consumed. This vicious cycle of energy consumption puts Proof of Work in an environmentally unfriendly situation. Thus, many seek viable alternatives to it. In this connection, Proof of Stake has emerged as another very popular way of reaching distributed consensus.

Proof of Stake is another way to determine value, but it has a much lower cost of input. Put in simple English, this approach can be summarized as "the rich get richer." Under Proof of Stake, the more Bitcoins you possess, the better the chance you are going to be assigned to solve the block. In Proof of Stake, miners are called validators. Validators need to deposit a certain amount of cryptocoins to start with. The more they deposit, the better chance they have to solve the new block. Proof of Stake does not need as much as electricity as traditional mining, and it's catching on. For example, Ethereum recently switched from Proof of Work to Proof of Stake.

WHY DIGITAL CURRENCY IS IMPORTANT

I've never been to Yap, an island in Micronesia, but I've heard that the money there is unique. Islanders on Yap use discs made from limestone as currency. If a disc is too big to move around—as many are—the owner has only to make a mark on that stone to indicate it has been used to settle a transaction. This is actually a somewhat similar concept to Bitcoin, at least in terms of how each transaction is documented.

Marking on a Yap stone disc is not much different from keeping transaction information preserved in a blockchain. The exchange information for Bitcoins (and other cryptocurrencies) is not kept in one central server. Rather, every transaction is documented in each block of a chain. The blockchain spreads out and runs on millions of computers, which makes it hard for anyone to hack, since it is not being kept on any single large database. Rather, the information is everywhere, all at the same time. In this way, blockchain is open and accessible to everyone in the Internet at any time. Privacy—at least in terms of spending and receiving money—is protected by use of the public and private keys. So Bitcoin is the asset of choice for the Internet, and the blockchain is the backbone protecting it by documenting and securing every single transaction.

It's been a decade since Satoshi laid down his vision for Bitcoin and Blockchain. From the early days of cypherpunks and tech nerds circulating a trendy new currency for insiders only, cryptocurrencies are now empowering the general public by providing a new way of participating in and conducting transactions. It may take a while for any cryptocurrency to rival traditional currency, but the idea is no longer science fiction. It could actually happen within our lifetimes. And if it does, we will realize new efficiencies in all kinds of transactions by undercutting third parties, creating fewer transaction costs, saving time, enjoying better security and safety, and preserving near-total anonymity.

Blockchain, separated from Bitcoin purely as a technology, is the next Internet.

The Internet brought us into the computer age (or information age) by making everything instant and available at the click of a mouse. Thanks to the Internet, the world has become flat. Communication across great distances is fast and equal.

Blockchain is going to enable us to embrace an even better and more connected world. It will be a world of trustworthiness through transparency, of information 24/7, and of increased openness that allows everybody to be involved. Blockchain opens the gate to new inventions and innovations, new applications, and youthful energy from the next generation.

It's new to many of us, and it's also very exciting. With just a bit more patience, I believe we're going to see blockchain unfold even further in important ways during the very near future

2.

Blockchain Evolving— From 1.0 to 2.0

I'm not a big fan of the violence in the HBO series *Westworld*, but I have to confess my appreciation for its efforts to explore the potential conflicts between the robotic hosts and the humans who create them.

In *Westworld*, robot hosts in a futuristic amusement park have one purpose and one purpose alone—to amuse the guests who pay handsomely for the experience. The robots are fully pro-grammed to fulfill the guests' desires in every way possible. Yet after a certain period of time, some of the robotic hosts begin to develop a consciousness and sense of self that goes beyond their programming. The first season of the show features the robots fighting for their freedom, and also fighting to define themselves existentially.

Will machines ever actually take over the world? Perhaps no one can say for sure. But the machines we create today are—on many levels—no different from the crude tools that were being created in the first days of human civilization. What they share is an attempt to push the present into the future in hopes of creat-ing something better. We are giving more power to the machine, and in return, we hope that the machine will make our lives eas-ier and better.

At this stage, we have probably passed a "point of no return" when it comes to relying on technology. Blockchain does not exist if there is no power to supply computers, or if there is no access to computers themselves. But is this really such a problem? To be honest, can we really live without our smartphones for a day? Technically, yes. But we'll probably feel terrible. We will want our smartphones back. We are dependent on the machines and the technology we have created, and that's okay.

Can you imagine the lives people had in the early 19th century before electricity was available? Can you even imagine life before people had TV? What about life before the Internet, smartphones, social media, and search engines? While many of you reading this may be able to remember that last one, would you actually want to live like that once more? Really?

We cannot go back. We must march forward with technology.

In this chapter, we will look at the evolution of blockchain, which I believe is sort of the "next step of the Internet."

If digital money was a gesture toward advancing the existing currency system, Bitcoin was the real breakthrough. Blockchain supports Bitcoin (and other cryptocurrencies) by storing all the transaction information into the chain (to avoid double spending and provide total transparency). It is also a decentralizing force that reshapes the power structure of regulation.

Essentially, blockchain is a database, a database that's distributed throughout the world instead of held on a central server. All transactions put into the block are validated by all the notes in the blockchain. It eliminates the need for trust by providing verification. It is impossible to change a block in the blockchain once is it created (and added to the public chain). Therefore, to fool the blockchain, you would need to control over 51 percent of the notes—a feat that could technically be done, but whose cost would be unbearable.

THE TYPES OF BLOCKCHAIN

Depending on its uses, blockchain can be placed into one of three categories: a public blockchain, a private blockchain, or a consortium blockchain.

A public blockchain is basically open to everyone in the world. Everyone can participate in it and can and be part of the validation process for transactions. Data on a public blockchain are likewise accessible to everyone. Reaching a distributed consensus on this type of blockchain makes the whole system run transparently and securely. Examples of public blockchains are Bitcoin and Ethereum.

Private blockchains, in contrast, are usually built by large companies for their own use alone. In contrast to a public blockchain (which runs without the need for trust), a private blockchain relies very much on trust among authorized people who have been granted access. Unlike the decentralization offered with a public blockchain, this type of blockchain is centralized, with access provided only to a limited number of users. You might think of this category as a kind of customized "blockchain on demand." Many different institutes and organizations have designed private blockchains based on their unique needs and will continue to do so in the future.

Finally, a consortium blockchain is a sort of subtype of private blockchain. You might say that it's in between a public blockchain and a private blockchain—partially decentralized. It enables two companies to share data that have been separately saved on each private blockchain.

These three types of blockchains find their best uses in different situations. Public blockchain creates a decentralized environment for information to flow without barriers. Private blockchain and consortium blockchains are more efficient in terms of privacy and purpose but are most applicable to organizations and companies that need their information made available only within certain limits.

SMART CONTRACT

So far, we've covered the basics of Bitcoin and blockchain. I hope I've given you the general sense that the blockchain for Bitcoin is sort of the "first generation" of blockchain. We could call it Blockchain 1.0. Ethereum and the smart contract are pushing blockchain into the next stage: Blockchain 2.0. Smart contract is critical to applying blockchain into broader use, so let's explore it further.

The computer scientist and cryptographer Nick Szabo first proposed the smart contract concept in a paper published in 1994. (It is worth noting that Szabo has been bandied about as the possible true identity of Satoshi, something he has denied.)

The smart contract created by Szabo is a computer system designed to facilitate and verify contracts between parties and people. The cryptocurrency Ethereum is a decentralized platform that runs smart contracts and allows developers to build their apps on the blockchain created by Ethereum. Smart contract is key in Ethereum, since it finally allows cryptocurrencies to be used in broader business activities. Smart contract can function in the absence of trust, because it executes terms without intervention from the parties involved. Once a smart contract is generated, it cannot be reversed. Transactions are traceable but irreversible. A smart contract works on an "if-then" language. If A happens, then B will take place. So once a contract is set up, the terms will be executed automatically.

Vending Machine—"A Physical Smart Contract"

An example often used to help explain smart contracts is a vending machine. Everyone knows how they work. You go to a vending machine and put in a certain amount of money; in return, the machine dispenses a product.

Say a vending machine sells sodas for $.25. Bob puts a quarter into the machine, and in return, it spits out a soda. Alice puts a dollar into the same machine, and it spits back $.75 and a soda.

Not a hard concept, right?

Well, smart contract on blockchain functions similarly.

Smart contract on blockchain involves three steps:

1. Parties involved in the contract reach a consensus and formulate a smart contract.
2. The parties put the contract into the blockchain through a peer-to-peer network.

3. The smart contract is put into motion once it's accepted into the blockchain.

Let's look at a real-world example. Say I would like to lease my apartment to you. You, as renter, pay me an advance in Bitcoins through a blockchain. Once the transaction is done, I receive the payment. You will then get a contract and receipt. And I, as landlord, will give you a key to enter the apartment within a certain period of time. If the key is not delivered to you on time, the blockchain will return the advance to you. If the key is delivered before the agreed date, the blockchain will temporarily hold the key until you pay the advance.

The system works on these if-then propositions, and everyone on the blockchain is able to see the contract we've both agreed upon. Therefore, nobody has to worry about the authenticity of the contract. And after the rental period is over, the contract will be automatically terminated once the terms have been fulfilled.

Just as Bitcoin is decentralizing currency and business transactions, smart contract has the potential to decentralize the entire contract market. Assets in digital format are now able to be exchanged and traded in blockchain by adopting smart contract, so all kinds of interesting trades can happen on blockchain. Smart contract broadens the potential use of blockchain dramatically—potentially bringing in almost the entire contractual landscape. And in my opinion, it's just getting started.

ETHEREUM: REDEMPTION AND BIRTH OF BLOCKCHAIN 2.0

Vitalik Buterin is a name almost everyone in computer science, blockchain, and cryptocurrency is familiar with. His white paper, "Ethereum: A Next-Generation Cryptocurrency and Decentralized Application Platform," released in *Bitcoin Magazine* back in 2014, put him into the spotlight. At just 19 years old, he totally disrupted the existing crypto world.

One way to understand his innovation—Ethereum—is to appreciate how it aims to replace third parties on the Internet through the use of blockchain. What are third parties on the Internet? They're services like Google, Facebook, and Apple that hold our personal data, financial data, and professional data on their servers. The importance of replacing third parties is all about security. Third parties makes it easier for hackers to hack, since everyone's data are all in one place (or in just a few places). Also, under a third-party system, governments may be able to access your files without your knowledge.

Ethereum is an open software platform based on blockchain technology that developers can use to build and deploy decentralized applications. The first generation of applications on blockchain is, admittedly, quite limited. The blockchain Bitcoin uses merely focuses on transactions (and tracking of transactions) using Bitcoins. The use of first-generation blockchain is also very narrowly defined. However, Ethereum is offering a public blockchain that goes beyond a peer-to-peer electronic cash system. By implementing smart contracts, the use of blockchain has the potential to expand beyond cryptocurrency. Anything of value can now be exchanged with and through smart contracts. Agreements and exchanges of every sort can theoretically run on Ethereum.

Apps built using Ethereum are called DAPPs. Developers create their DAPPs using smart contracts. In keeping with the theme of decentralization, DAPPs are all decentralized and are not owned by individuals or organizations. Rather, they are owned by multiple people—specifically, everyone on blockchain.

Despite these innovations, it hasn't all been wine and roses. In the short history of Ethereum so far, it's had several major challenges. Probably, the biggest has been the DAO.

In May of 2016, the former CCO of Ethereum, Stephan Tual, founded Slock.it, along with a few members of the Ethereum team. In doing so, he also announced the concept of the DAO—the Decentralized Autonomous Organization. Despite very little information about what the DAO actually was, during its Initial Coin

Offering (ICO), the DAO raised an amount of Ethereum equal to $150 million from over 20,000 investors.

However, on June 17, 2016, a hacker hacked the DAO through a loophole in the system. Within just a couple of hours, the DAO lost 3.6 million ETH, the equivalent of $70 million. The loophole facilitating this hacking did not come from Ethereum itself, but from an application on which it was built. However, the resulting mess was left to the Ethereum team and community to take care of. Several proposals were presented to get the stolen money back. Because transferred funds were always held in an account for twenty-eight days, the hacker couldn't simply take the money and run. Ethereum eventually proposed to "hardfork" the funds to an account available to the original owners. A hardfork involves making a primordial change to blockchain that can make previously invalid transactions valid, or vice versa. But by doing so, it subverts the shared goal of decentralization that so many people involved in cryptocurrency share. Eventually, even though 10 percent of the Ethereum community voted against it, Ethereum decided to hardfork 192 million blocks in order to retrieve the stolen funds. After this was done, a new blockchain was created called ETH (separate from the original blockchain, ETC).

There are many takeaways for the cryptocurrency and blockchain communities that come out of the DAO incident. If you're interested in getting granular, there are many articles on Google. However, as Einstein is supposed to have said, a person who never made a mistake is a person who never tried anything new. Smart contracts is something new, and so is everything related to blockchain. In my opinion, there are going to be bumps in the road—like DAO—along the way. But as long as we survive and learn from our mistakes, we shall all be stronger in the end.

THE TRADITIONAL FINANCIAL MARKET REBORN

Smart contracts have been widely adopted across the digital world. Almost all active ICO projects are now using smart contracts. Tokens and the ownership of tokens will also always be written into a smart contract. For example, in a typical ICO, 10 percent of tokens are reserved to the ICO team, 50 percent of tokens go to private investors, and 40 percent go to public investors. And all of these conditions will be written into the smart contract, which is accessible to everyone in the community. Thus, once the ICO goes public, the smart contract will be put in motion to execute the terms automatically.

Smart contracts are expanding into other areas, as well. Clyde & Co. is a global law firm that recently formed a team to provide consulting services to clients who would like to set up smart contracts from technical, as well as legal, perspectives. And one of the world's largest insurance companies, AXA, recently announced the launch of Fizzy, the very first insurance product using both blockchain technology and smart contracts. (Fizzy mainly provides insurance covering flight delays.)

In October of 2017, Ernst & Young collaborated with blockchain developer Guardtime to explore applying blockchain to the marine insurance sector. PwC and Northern Trust announced an instant blockchain auditing service early this year. (PwC will be providing private equity auditors with instant access to data stored on a private blockchain.) In traditional auditing, auditors receive periodic reports from clients, which is not always an efficient way of doing things. But by having near-instant access to the data regarding actions taken by a fund manager (for example), the whole process can be audited in real time.

THE FUTURE OF SMART CONTRACTS

I'm confident that in the future, smart contracts will be put into even broader use in the financial sector. I think this for a number of reasons. To go back to PwC: in PwC's distributed accounting reports, there is now a thorough analysis of the future of blockchain and smart contracts. Since a smart contract is capable of self-executing contracts related to assets transfer, it, as a technology, definitely presents uses related to stock trading and other financial market trading.

Another reason for the growth of smart contracts will be the growth of the Internet of Things (IoT). According to Gartner Inc., the global research firm, worldwide IoT security spending will reach $1.5 billion in 2018. By 2021, it is expected to climb to $3.1 billion. Everything around us, including smartphones, cars, wearable products, and even furniture, is going to be connected to the Internet. This will create exponential data needs. What will we use to capture and store all of these new data? Blockchain.

Another trend in smart contracts' favor is that blockchain is cost-efficient and friendly. In traditional law firms and auditing firms, adopting blockchain and smart contracts will significantly lower the cost of doing business and improve efficiency. It will be a win-win.

ICO: BUBBLE OR EXTRA BONUS?

Ethereum brought ICO to startups as a new way to raise capital. Ethereum announced its own ICO on September 2, 2014, and it placed among the top five of all time in terms of the sheer amount of capital it raised. Ethereum raised $18.4 million, most of which was spent developing Ethereum blockchain and related applications. (The record for "largest ICO" has been consistently broken. The EOS cryptocurrency's token sales reached $4.1 billion over a one-year ICO, making it, for the moment, the number one ICO in history.)

The evolution of ICOs has happened in two stages. In the early days, speculators who hoped to make fast money were always there to try to take advantage of the situation somehow. An ICO is, of course, not a Ponzi scheme, but rather a way for blockchain startups to raise money. But ICOs can be initiated by unsavory people who are only in it for quick profits at the expense of other people. These days, there is more awareness of this danger. However, in the early days of ICOs, token sales were always great, but some of them were being sold by scammers. In the second stage—the one we're in now—as ICOs evolve into something more professional and transparent, they are attracting individuals and institutions from the traditional financial industry. There are advantages to this, yes, but it can also make things more standardized and slow things down. Blockchain, as an industry, is gathering experts and high-profile managers from across traditional industries and is improving every day and every hour.

I believe that an ICO is soon going to be as accepted as an IPO is today. People make mistakes when they are young, and so do institutions. This was certainly true with ICOs. However, they have now become more consolidated and established. Launching an ICO is now as demanding as launching an IPO. It involves nearly everything that an IPO requires. Cryptocurrency and block-chain are interlinked so closely. Cryptocurrencies are supporting blockchain startups, and blockchain startups are relying on tokens to be issued and token sales to raise capital to grow bigger. At the same time, both are learning from traditional industries as well as bringing the latter more fully into the crypto economy.

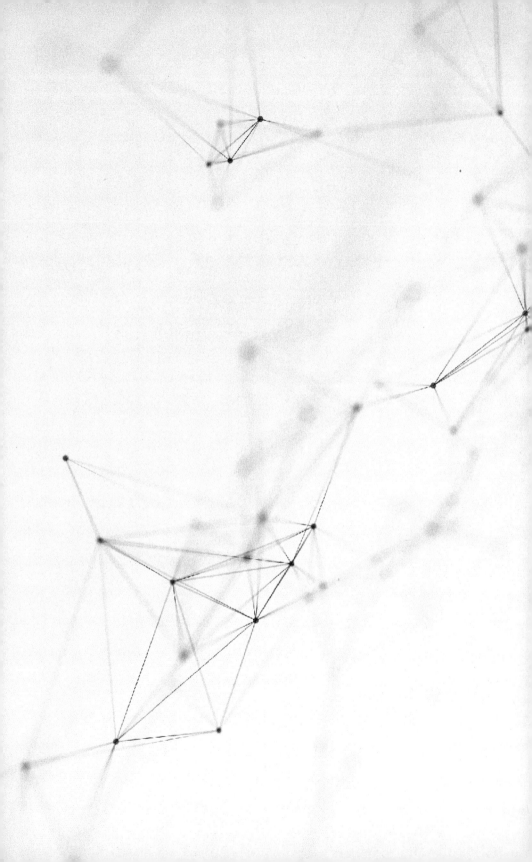

3.

GOLD RUSH—TODAY'S MINING OPPORTUNITY

In 1848, after a local newspaper whispered that gold had been found in certain rivers in California, about 300,000 people from across United States left their homes and rushed west to follow their dreams of getting rich.

The consequences were unexpected and the effects substantial. When the California Gold Rush took off in March of 1848, California was not even a state yet. (It makes me wonder what made Uncle Sam let California into the family: maybe the fact that approximately 3,700 tons of gold have been retrieved from the bottom of its rivers!)

History often repeats itself. Today, mining Bitcoin has become another Gold Rush. When Satoshi first "discovered" Bitcoin, he set a ceiling on the number of Bitcoins that could ever exist: 21 million units. And every four years, 210,000 new Bitcoins are released into the system. As the most valuable cryptocurrency, many people can't wait to get into Bitcoin mining. But how precisely does it work? Instead of picking up a pan, as most forty-niners did in California's Gold Rush, miners of Bitcoin use a far more sophisticated tool to dig for gold.

Satoshi created a decentralized network accessible through an open-source software available to everyone. In this network, people use Bitcoins to make exchanges. In order to avoid the double spending issue, Satoshi introduced blockchain, which will document every single transaction that happens, has ever happened, or is ever going to happen. But blockchain does not create itself. It depends on computer processing power to generate new blocks into the chain and maintain the system function. This is the true purpose of mining. Bitcoins are the reward for miners who either create new blocks or input transaction information into blockchain.

In order to become a miner, a person needs to join blockchain and get connected with other nodes. Once the connection is fully established, miners will need to fulfill six tasks:

1. Listen for transactions.
2. Listen for new blocks and maintain blockchain. If there is a new block, the miner needs to validate it.
3. Assemble a new valid block based on the transactions the miner has been hearing.
4. Find a nonce—*a.k.a.* an arbitrary number that can be used only once—to make the block valid.
5. Hope everyone in blockchain accepts the new block.
6. Enjoy profits! If everyone accepts the new block, the miner will be rewarded accordingly.

Miners need to validate new blocks (which means new transactions are coming into the network). This is the most critical work when it comes to maintaining the circulation of Bitcoin. But they also have to create new blocks, an activity that can be strikingly competitive. Miners compete with one another for new blocks. This part is not necessary to maintain the whole system of Bitcoin, but it functions as the incentive to encourage miners to fulfill the validation part of a job.

When Satoshi invented Bitcoin, he introduced this "motivating mechanism" to encourage miners to maintain the function of blockchain. But since the total number of Bitcoins is 21 million and only 210,000 Bitcoins are released every four years, the reward halves accordingly. Thus, in 2009, the reward was 50 Bitcoins in a block. But by 2016, it was down to 12.5 Bitcoins for each new block. When all Bitcoins are released into the system, the reward will drop to zero.

Even though the financial reward for creating new blocks is going away, the transaction fee remains an incentive to attract miners. In blockchain, users will be charged a certain fee in order to broadcast and document each transaction. The fee then goes to the miners who will put the information into the blocks. This generates a "bidding system." Bidding happens when there are many transactions waiting to be put into blocks. The higher a transaction fee you are willing to pay, the better chance you have of jumping ahead in the waiting line. As the fee for completing transactions keeps going up, miners will keep becoming more important in the world blockchain and cryptocurrency. (Miners are similar to the programmers working at Internet companies who maintain functions.)

Launched on May 21, 2018, a China-based cryptocurrency exchange called FCoin has proposed a new business model called "Trans-Fee Mining." This effectively turns the cryptotrading itself into mining. For each transaction fee that users pay FCoin on its platform (in Bitcoin or Ethereum), users will be compensated 100 percent in FTs (a token issued by FCoin). Meanwhile, the platform will also allocate 80 percent of the transaction fee to FTs holders.

This model immediately boosted energy and created excitement among traders. Since trading and mining are the same thing on FCoin, if you trade on FCoin, the transaction fee is zero. But if you own FTs, you will be able to share the 80 percent of transaction fees generated from the platform proportional to the amount of FTs you hold. (This model has been defined by some as a "Token Economy.")

Since FCoin's launch, the volume of its trades has increased rapidly. Based on the success of the Trans-Fee Mining model, more and more new exchanges have come into the game. Users seem to love the approach to reimbursement and reward. However, the model itself has been criticized, with some alleging that "trans-fee mining" is just another form of ICO scheme.

Despite the criticism of the model, I think introducing a new rewarding system into blockchain is laudable and encourages people to explore the possibilities of using different reward methods.

In the "Gold Rush" of Bitcoin, miners are trying their best to mine new blocks before others can, and many miners are now forced to tolerate a very high level of risk. Satoshi created the first block. (People call it "the genius block.") And every single block generated afterward is linked back to it. Blockchain is continuously growing as new transactions take place. But as I mentioned earlier, the fundamental architecture of blockchain requires a great amount of computing power. Computing power determines the speed of the mining, and the speed of the mining determines who is going be rewarded with Bitcoins for creating the next block faster than everyone else.

One of effects of the California Gold Rush was the improvement of gold-recovery techniques. At the beginning of the Gold Rush, because the gold was so richly concentrated in the gravel bed, using hands or pans or anything you could find in the kitchen was enough for forty-niners to retrieve those loose gold flakes and nuggets. But as more and more people joined in the search for their own California Dream, the tools had to become more advanced. In the first five years of Gold Rush, about 370 tons of gold were recovered—mostly by people digging with their hands. But from then until today, only about 3,700 tons of gold have been recovered in California. Getting gold got much harder as time went by.

The same has held true with Bitcoin mining; early birds get more worms. A simple personal computer was enough for miners in the early stages. But now, the cost of input has increased significantly because mining demands consolidated resources. Putting aside the cost of the mining machine itself, just keeping a mining machine going can cost an enormous amount in electricity fees.

China has drawn a lot of attention in this connection from people looking at maps of electricity consumption.

China is not only known for mining, but also as a leading computer chip manufacturer. It's estimated that over 80 percent of cryptocurrencies have been mined using computer chips manufactured in mainland China. Bitmain Technologies Ltd. (or Bitmain), with headquarters in Beijing, is the largest producer of Bitcoin mining chips in the world. According to Business Insider, Bitmain's founder, the cryptocurrency billionaire Jihan Wu, told Bloomberg that Bitmain was considering an initial public offering as it expands into producing hardware for artificial-intelligence computing.

THE CHANGING VALUE OF BITCOINS

Here's a related question: if you are a miner, after you get your Bitcoins—either through transaction fees or creating new blocks—what do you do with them?

You'd be surprised how the answer has changed over time.

On May 22, 2010, Laszlo Hanyeca, a computer programmer, bought two pizzas for the low, low price of only 10,000 Bitcoins. The purchase is widely considered to be the first transaction in the history of Bitcoin. As of the writing of this book, these two pizzas would be worth about $75 million, making them the most expensive pizzas in history.

From $20,000 per Bitcoin down to about $6,000, Bitcoin has been on a heck of ride recently. Ethereum, the second most valuable cryptocurrency, stands at $453.93 per unit at the time of this writing. And overall users of cryptocurrencies have increased from around 30,000 just a few years ago to over 1.3 million. So despite fluctuations in the market, there's evidence that the public is increasingly accepting of cryptocurrency.

The extreme up-and-down fluctuation we see in cryptocurrency trading prices corresponds to the confidence (or lack of it) that people hold in these currencies. The overall amount of a cryptocurrency is always fixed. If the demand-supply works effectively for cryptocurrency, more investment will always come in. It's the same idea with gold, diamonds, or works of art. The market sometimes sees the value of cryptocurrency as uncertain, but confidence overall continues to grow as more people become comfortable with the idea. Bitcoin has, of course, experienced extreme fluctuations in value. Yet, as time goes by, I'm confident the public will continue to develop better understandings of exchange platforms for cryptocurrencies. They will become more typical, "normal," and accepted, which will, in turn, help the value of cryptocurrencies overall.

The attitude of the government also plays a huge role in determining the future value of a cryptocurrency. Though the technology of crypto is designed for decentralization—the opposite of what has been going on with currency for thousands of years—the opinion of a central government can still push things one way or the other (even if it feels left out). In the United States, some government officials and entities have issued consumer warnings regarding cryptocurrencies. Yet they've also said that cryptos are legal and should be allowed to exist. In some circles, this has counted as an endorsement of sorts.

This brings us to the question of how to stabilize the value of cryptocurrency in the future. It's an important issue that will need to be resolved soon.

Dominant cryptocurrencies—such as Bitcoin and Ethereum—have already gained acceptance and (eventually) steady valuation. But not all cryptos have been as lucky. Almost a decade after the birth of Bitcoin, there are more and more people who are using, and investing in, Bitcoin, and it has been treated as a digital asset of great value globally. Along with Ethereum, Bitcoin has been seen as one of the strongest currencies in the world of cryptocurrency. In June of 2018, in an informal statement made at Yahoo Finance's "All Markets Summit Crypto," the SEC's director of finance stated that the SEC would not classify Bitcoin or Etherium as a security. Rather, the official said, both cryptocurrencies function more like commodities such as gold, silver, or oil. Will a decentralized cryptocurrency ever overtake a traditionally defined currency in status or value? It's hard to tell at this point. But with more and more activities and transactions happening online, the chance to cut out middlemen, use smart contracts, and purchase merchandise with cryptocurrency may be a temptation too strong to resist. With all the cost-effectiveness it is bringing us, I believe cryptocurrency will play a bigger and bigger role in all manner of scenarios.

ICO—INITIAL COIN OFFERING – THE NEW IPO

Throughout most of recent history, an IPO has been the standard path for companies to attract investors through selling stocks. However, the process involves banks and venture capitalists who stand to make money on fees. An ICO undercuts intermediaries, such as venture capitalists and banks, removing them from the fundraising process.

In Chapter 2, we briefly talked about Ethereum's misadventure with the very first ICO on its platform, the DAO. I hope I can make the case to you here that times have changed since then, and that ICOs have changed. While they once felt like a Kickstarter or Indiegogo campaign, they now have about them the sober propriety of an IPO and then some.

During 2017, using ICOs, blockchain startups raised about $7 billion. Compare that to the capital raise of only $1 billion enjoyed by traditional VC for blockchain startups during that period. I think this makes the case that the ICO model is increasingly trusted, and also very hot. Over 200 ICOs have raised in excess of $10M—with many going vastly above that. EOS, a blockchain system for supporting central business districts, attracted $4 billion; Filecoin took in $257 million; Tezos raised $232 million; and Bancor Protocol locked in $153 million.

The money changing hands in these ICOs has drawn a decent amount of attention from SEC. Mostly, these ICOs remain unregulated by the government. Some consumer advocates claim the rules are not clear when it comes to how investors will be properly protected. In June of 2018, the Chairman of the SEC, Jay Clayton, was interviewed by CNBC. In this interview, he stated that tokens and ICOs were securities. This issue is changing moment to moment, but based on these comments, it is reasonable to believe that ICOs will probably one day fall under SEC regulation to a greater degree.

Yet there is always an alternative when regulation is forced upon us. The American startups that are looking for an ICO are learning from the Chinese Internet companies that typically raise capital overseas now. The MIIT (Ministry of Industry and Information Technology) and Press and Publication Administration of China have stated that an Internet license can only be held by domestically funded companies. However, US-based startups are learning from these Chinese work-arounds when launching their ICOs. For example, let's say that a domestic-based American company, Company A, is planning to launch an ICO. Company A will set up Company C in a cryptically friendly country. And another company, Company B, will be established to operate the ICO. But Company C will technically be the parent company of both A and B.

Perhaps such attention is being paid to ICOs because of the speculators in the market who, looking for a quick gain, had taken advantage of the unregulated system in its earliest days. Yet as more pump-and-dump schemes popped up in the ICO world, a self-cleansing mechanism was triggered. Investment banks, financial services providers, and technology companies based in Silicon Valley joined in to filter and vet projects looking for an ICO. The combination of all these forces raised the entry barrier by filtering out the unqualified or sketchy deals.

Any project going for an ICO is now being examined closely by multiple entities. Endorsements from qualified individuals or institutions are not given lightly. Further, the time frame of an ICO has been extended, allowing investors more time to conduct their due diligence. And overall, the procedure for launching an ICO has become more standardized.

Perhaps some resistance should not be surprising. After all, the ICO is challenging the existing capital-raising format. Because it is more barrier-free than typical VC raises, people are jumping in. While not all ICOs have been successful—and, yes, some have been scams—there are many blockchain startups that have been wildly successful under the ICO model. The vast majority of these businesses are trying their best to bring genuine value to people's daily lives through the world of blockchain.

There are good apples, and there are bad apples. This will always be true. We cannot cut down the tree whenever a bad apple pops up. It would be unfair to the good ones. Yes, the ICO model probably needs a little bit more time to evolve into the best version of itself. Yet even in its current form, it can defend investors and offer great ideas and projects.

Martin Chen, founder of GDP Capital, a New York-based consulting firm, believes that most Internet-based services are suitable for an ICO. Blockchain and cryptocurrencies are born on the Internet, and they share the same "genes"—you might say—in that they both connect one person to another in a truly open world. In a token-centered community, information regarding the total number of tokens to be issued is always transparent and certain. Everyone in the community has access to this information, and the value of the token will go up as more and more people join that community. Obviously, there are tremendous benefits to this model. For the foreseeable future, I think it's reasonable to believe that token-centered communities will prove themselves superior to a traditional stock-based model.

Regionally imposed restrictions now have less of an influence on ICOs. Because of this, more and more Chinese companies seeking to go public are considering an ICO instead of an IPO. ICOs, through token sales, introduce firm advantages of liquidity to the stock. For many companies, an ICO is also appealing because it undercuts (or eliminates entirely) the costs and complicated paperwork usually involved in an IPO. Further, an ICO does not require companies to "open their books" to reveal their existing business performance. Many owners find this makes them more comfortable with the ICO model.

Have no doubt about it, the ICO is designed to challenge the traditional VC model. Yet whenever a company is in the process of launching an ICO, nothing prevents a venture capitalist from buying tokens and becoming a part of that community. In a way, this can open up new possibilities for traditional VC investors. For example, the valuation of a company is not restricted to the decrees or findings of a few specialized institutions but is based on the consensus of the whole community. The ICO model also offers solutions and opportunities for companies in industries that are usually ignored by VC.

Because the value of a company is determined by the whole community under the ICO model, we can see the promulgation of this model as another blow for decentralization (and against a small cluster of powerful regulating bodies). However, it will always be pointed out that subverting the power of traditional regulating institutions has been a double-edged sword—or at least it was in the early days of ICOs. Eight or nine years ago, there were definitely speculators who got in the game solely to rook people. Projects and companies turned out to be scams and schemes. This forced ICO investors to collectively become more savvy, and the learning curve was quick. But these early leaks did not sink the ship.

ICOs are also popular because they hold the potential for remarkably superior ROI (Return On Investment) when compared to other offerings. With traditional VC investments, it usually takes ten years to get one's initial investment back and then realize a profit. The rapid growth in blockchain and cryptocurrency has made this time horizon a relic of the past. In the world of blockchain, things move quickly. Things happen, and they don't stop to take a break. The energy is young and wild. Opportunities are everywhere. Investors now understand that people need to move fast in this world if they want to catch the early train before it leaves the platform—and cash in on the benefits of being an early investor. In today's climate, it usually takes fewer than twenty-four hours for a major American fund to finish an investment deal made through an ICO. This is a remarkable change, and it isn't going to reverse itself anytime soon.

THE TRADITIONAL FINANCIAL INDUSTRY
TRIES . . . SOMETHING NEW

Have you ever used a dating app?

In a lot of ways, blockchain now faces the same conundrum as a new "hot date" on Tinder. You could say that blockchain is receiving all kinds of "winks" and "likes" from traditional financial institutions. But are they ready to make a true connection and go out for coffee in real life? That remains to be seen. Relevant financial products are being developed by these institutions—especially when it comes to Bitcoin—but it may just be the equivalent of flirting on Tinder after a couple of cocktails.

In December of 2017, the Chicago Mercantile Exchange launched the the first trading instruments for Bitcoin futures. Yet so far, no European countries have followed suit and provided any Bitcoin or cryptocurrency-related financial products. Deutsche Boerse AG, the parent company of the Frankfurt Stock Exchange, appears to have begun work on a technology that will allow them to offer their clients Bitcoin and cryptocurrency-related products, but it remains in the early stages.

Back in the US, after rejecting the Winklevoss brothers' initial application for a Bitcoin Exchange-Traded Fund (ETF), the SEC has made statements recently that hint it may be changing its tune on the idea. If one thing is sure, it's that we're at a juncture in which governments' attitudes toward Bitcoin and crypto are largely unknowable—and if they are known, they're revealed to vary widely from country to country. Some countries are very friendly when it comes to crypto, and some are the opposite. In Germany, for example, Bitcoin is now technically a "legal tender," meaning that Bitcoin is allowed to be used for tax purposes and for commercial trading. In the United States, Bitcoin can be used like regular money in many situations—and many businesses accept it—but it is *not* considered to be legal tender by the IRS. However, as we all know, this doesn't mean the IRS isn't "interested" in your Bitcoins. They are *very* interested. Bitcoins are considered to be your personal property, just like gold or a house, which means they have to comply with tax codes. According to the IRS, the value of a Bitcoin for US tax purposes is its fair market value in US dollars on the date it is received, and any transaction fees are added to that. If a person is trading Bitcoins as capital assest, then the gain is supposed to be taxed at capital gains rate.

As the appeal of crypto pushes the door wider and wider, traditional investment banks are catching on to the game. According to the *New York Times*, Goldman Sachs is about to open a Bitcoin trading operation on Wall Street. The operation will not buy or sell Bitcoins directly but is rather designed to meet the needs of their clients who may be exploring investments in cryptocurrency. Wall Street has generally shied away from Bitcoin and cryptocurrencies, but Goldman's decision to dip its toe in the water may be a bellwether. In a recent interview, Rana Yared, an executive involved in creating these offerings, said that Goldman Sachs "had concluded Bitcoin is not a fraud." Many clients of Goldman Sachs consider Bitcoin a commodity of value, and Goldman knows this. Because the amount of Bitcoins is forever set, a comparison to a commodity like gold makes sense for Goldman's clients. There is a finite amount of gold in the world. Barring an innovation by alchemists, there will never be more than there is right now. This connection to something real and finite is probably the quality that most makes Goldman comfortable moving forward.

For today's crypto "true believers," the appeal extends beyond the fact that big banks may have found Bitcoin semipalatable. Many users, including some Goldman clients, genuinely believe that blockchain is doing something good for the future of commerce and humanity. There are others who have no larger ideological drive but would simply like to sit at the table when the pie is being shared. If we're being frank, the investment banks probably fall into this latter group. But that doesn't mean their participation in growing the presence of crypto will not be meaningful or important.

There's a saying I like: "Get busy living or get busy dying."

I like this precisely because it helps me wrap my mind around the forces driving crypto today. Those with faith in the currency have chosen to get busy promoting it, using it, and sharing it. They believe that it can help us go further and help our economic system become better. I think that's an inspiring view!

If you see blockchain as something inevitable—something that's going to happen whether banks and governments like it or not— then doubt in the marketplace can only be viewed as the age-old fear of change. If you see blockchain as an extension of how the Internet reached us and became a vital part of our lives—whether we wanted it to or not—then the eventual success of blockchain feels assured. And it also indicates that those who fail to evolve and accept blockchain may well fail to survive the future that is coming.

Blockchain is young. So is cryptocurrency, and so are ICOs. But I, along with many experts in the field, see blockchain as the foundation of our financial future. It's a future that's going to include cryptocurrencies, tokens, ICOs, smart contracts, and many other applications that haven't even been invented yet! But as all of these elements continue to function together and grow stronger, the ecosystem of the crypto economy seems like it will soon have too much momentum to fail.

4.

VOCEAN—DECENTRALIZING FINANCIAL SERVICES

Let's go back to 2008 again. The subprime mortgage crisis that flattened the economy that year proved a boon for storytellers, and not just in cryptocurrency books. I'm not sure if you've seen the 2011 movie *Margin Call*, but it's worth your time. I would especially recommend it if you're interested in the financial industry's (dys)function, and how profoundly it influences every aspect of our daily lives. The movie basically limns the situation immediately prior to the financial crisis. A risk-management analyst has caught a mistake and suddenly understands the hit that his industry is about to take—and what the impact may be for the rest of the world. The film is revealing because it lays bare the philosophy and attitude underpinning the whole of Wall Street, namely, that risk is usually not identified and acknowledged during times when the system seems to be working fine and everybody is making money. But as greed grows, things always spiral out of control. The financial industry manages trillions of dollars worth of assets. The whole world, in some fashion or another, relies on Wall Street to function correctly. When it doesn't, trust is shaken and everybody is impacted.

But what if there were new and different ways of doing things? What if there were new technologies that might allow us to avoid the Wall Street busts and crashes of the past?

I can happily report that some very smart people are trying to answer these very questions. And if early returns are any indication, it looks like they are making progress.

FROM OFFLINE BANKING TO BLOCKCHAIN BANKING

A new, New York-based company called Vocean is leading the way when it comes to connecting fixed-income financial instruments to blockchain. A recent white paper issued by the firm lays out the approach that Vocean intends to take, and the benefits to consumers. Essentially, Vocean seeks to create a decentralized lending platform and loan derivatives market that will allow for dynamic collateral management and disintermediated clearing. Using state-of-the-art blockchain technology, Vocean aims to provide assistance to investors managing digital assets, cryptoinvestments, and related financial products in the realm of the "token economy."

In order to understand how Vocean plans to navigate the tricky task of combining traditional financial services products with blockchain, we need to take a look at the role that debt plays in the financial industry.

There are many kinds of debt and debt-related financial instruments. They can come in the form of redeemable notes issued by a government, bonds issued by companies, mortgages, personal loans, student loans, and more. (Just use Wikipedia if you want to learn more about the basics of debt and financial instruments.) A debt generally also includes specific, contractual terms regarding the amount and timing of repayments (for example, your minimum credit card payment), and things like principal and interest. Almost all financial products used today find their roots in debt.

Vocean would like to use blockchain to increase the efficiency of the entire financial industry as it relates to the issuing of debt. The CEO of Vocean, Jerry Zhong, is not new to using technology to address financial problems. Zhong was one of the "early birds" back in early 1990s who jumped into the Internet with both feet. He sees the current upcoming wave of blockchain as very similar to the early stages of Internet adoption and sees where we are now as comparable to the period when people were trying to figure out how to push the Internet into broader use. There's no doubt that the Internet succeeded in connecting physical services (financial or otherwise) into online processes. This created efficiencies for everyone. According to visionaries like Zhong, the coming adoption of blockchain is going to migrate everything we do online onto blockchain, allowing us to achieve decentralization and realize new efficiency improvements. We stand at a juncture in which professionals in traditional industries are realizing this. They are preparing for the coming changes blockchain will bring, and they're getting creative with it whenever possible.

According to Vocean, the current financial industry has three key weak points. However, Vocean believes it will be able to introduce blockchain-based efficiencies that will address all three.

First, traditional banking services suffer from "low efficiency" management of their funds and records. The sheer amount of transactions they must record are huge. All too frequently, banking information is stored in different computer terminals, or on slow computer networks. Because of the information delays this creates, traders at investment banks are less able to make quick and fully informed decisions on behalf of their investors.

Second, financial service firms still need third parties to complete the clearinghouse function. A clearinghouse is a financial institution that facilitates the exchange of payments, securities, or derivatives. Essentially, it functions as a middleman connecting two firms. It also ensures that both firms honor their agreements and fulfill their obligations. You could view a clearinghouse as a kind of early-stage PayPal. PayPal provides not only a platform on which transactions can take place, but it also facilitates the transaction between the buyer and the seller. PayPal usually charges a 3 percent fee for its services, much like a clearinghouse. After the buyer submits a payment, PayPal will hold it temporarily and release it when the buyer confirms the receipt of the merchandise.

In the traditional financial marketplace, clearinghouses are necessary to reduce costs and mitigate operational risk.

The third problem Vocean can address is the need for security in cryptocurrency by means of a "custodian." Exchange desks and wallet services have not proven foolproof. Hacking incidents do happen from time to time. The resulting security and safety issues are a barrier for many large institutional investors. As long as they entertain the specter of "losing money because of a hack," they will be reluctant to do business related to blockchain or cryptocurrency. Yet the traditional financial industry has developed effective custodians for investors to help them store and manage their fiat money and traditional assets. JPMorgan Chase, State Street Bank, and Mellon Finance, for example, have been keeping in their custody billions of assets on behalf of other institutions for years. As crypto assets have increased, the need for similar custodian services has become clear. In May of 2018, Coinbase—an American Bitcoin exchange and wallet service platform—began providing its own version of custodian service. Adam White, the VP of Coinbase, says he is anticipating billions of institutional investment dollars in this connection. And according to the May 2018 issue of *Cointelegraph*, Nomura Bank, a Japanese financial institution, announced that it would begin providing a "crypto custody solution" for institutional investors. Nomura's venture will be conducted in partnership with digital asset security company Ledger and with the investment house Global Advisors. And according to a recent piece in the *New York Times*, ICE, the parent company of the NYSE, has been developing an online trading platform for Bitcoin SWAP.

Crypto custodian services present further evidence of forward momentum in the evolution of cryptocurrency. As it grows, cryptocurrency will, step by step, be accepted by, and necessitate the ability to interface with, broader financial services.

When it comes to these three sticking points, Vocean believes it can provide solutions *via* blockchain technologies. How are Vocean's solutions going to be different from what's being offered by traditional banking services? Foremost, Jerry Zhong believes that blockchain will greatly increase the efficiency of investing and all related financial services. A big part of this will be the use of smart contracts. Since the smart contract is irreversible, terms can (and will) be executed without human intervention. Things will be automatic. Further, all the data are stored on the public chain, which will be accessible to all parties involved in a transaction and which will considerably lower costs (especially when compared to the traditional price point of managing collateral posted to banks).

Vocean is moving forward by building upon the public chain made possible by Ethereum. Zhong has explained that his ultimate purpose is to maximize outcomes by minimizing the costs and time inputs associated with financial transactions. Vocean believes the infrastructure of Ethereum has been proved solid. The customers targeted by Vocean are financial institutions who put safety and privacy as the two issues at the top of their lists. Are there any trade-offs or challenges? The big one is speed. Currently, Ethereum can process fifteen transactions per second. That might sound like a lot, but Visa can put up about 45,000 transactions per second. Even so, Vocean believes this hurdle in manageable, and that speed will improve over time. Vocean is also constructing two smart contract systems. One smart contract system will manage the "borrow-lend" function, which connects borrowers, lenders, and mortgage management entities. Through the system, these three parties can execute semisimultaneous trades. The other smart contract system will serve the function of the clearinghouses we discussed above. Due to the complexity of the market, price is in a constant state of fluctuation and adjustment. Vocean is developing a specific smart contract to manage collateral in this environment. When a huge (up or down) price change triggers a margin call, the system will protect the value of assets and serve the best interests of credit holders.

Vocean will also work to enable cross-chain crypto transactions. In traditional financial situations, borrowers and lenders make exchanges across different currencies all the time. Bitcoin and Ether, however, are traded in separate public chains, and sadly, Ethereum does not support cross-chain crypto transactions. Vocean is planning to build an application to enable this service.

As I think you can see, Ethereum has become the fundamental infrastructure in much of the blockchain and cryptocurrency world. Despite its prevalence, it still isn't perfect. Blockchain can be seen as a data storage facility that offers a high level of security, but at the cost of low speed. It is not suitable for complicated logic functions, or for repeatable trades of low value. Vocean aims to balance its reliance on Ethereum with other in-chain and off-chain services. In so doing, it hopes to be able to provide the best of both worlds.

WAIT AND SEE

There is still a considerable amount of capital waiting outside the crypto door, looking inside to see if it's worth it to come in. There are estimated to be $20 billion in Bitcoins still to enter the market. Vocean is set to be ready when it does.

To get the money waiting outside the door comfortable enough to come inside, custodian service providers (usually, certain banks) will need to accomplish the goal of increasing the value of assets. Thus, designing low-risk, fixed-income investments is high on their list. When it comes to investment banks getting into the space, their concern is that they would need a considerable amount of crypto to offset risk and increase liquidity. Often, investment banks solve this issue using "swap and repo"—also known as a repurchase agreement. In a typical repurchase agreement, a dealer sells securities to a counterparty with the agreement to buy back the securities at a higher price at a later date. If the dealer borrows money, it is a repo. If the dealer lends money, it is a reverse repo. Once the crypto market becomes consolidated, there will be huge demand for these transactions using cryptocurrency. Vocean is designing a platform to assist custodian banks and investment banks in profiting from these transactions.

As investment banks and hedge funds start getting deeper into crypto assets, the demand for lenders and borrowers will increase.

Zhong predicts that within the next twelve months, custodian banks will become a very common sight in the crypto market. Clients who need custodian services—such as miners or mining farms—will be the holders of large amounts of cryptocurrency. They'll need reputable custodian services to safely take care of their crypto assets. According to a survey published by Reuters, one in five major financial institutions is currently considering trading cryptocurrency by the end of 2019. Vocean is ready for this market.

Vocean also plans to build an active investing platform (and corresponding online community) with the execution of three key steps. The first step is to build the platform and begin collaborating with custodian banks to migrate the asset. The second step will be to introduce already-existing financial products to a blockchain-based service. And the final step for Vocean will be to build a community of centralized investors to help address any issues that occur with investments.

Technically, trading is not going to happen "on Vocean," but off-chain. However, Vocean is building an AI system for lenders and borrowers in which the two will be matched by loan criteria. Such factors as ideal loan term, collateral/loan pair, collateral ratio, interest rate, and liquidation option will be used to connect the ideal lender to the ideal borrower. It will be a little like the algorithm of a good dating site that connects potential partners through their common interests.

Investors in the community will also be rated. Traders' investment performance and credit rating will be documented and posted into blockchain. This system will also analyze their trading behaviors. In addition, the platform will provide training and education-related services for investors to help them learn about risk management in crypto assets.

Blockchain innovations have been coming at us fast and furious. I don't expect the pace of innovation to stop, and I believe that each innovation will make the water feel warmer for traditional investors. But effectively applying blockchain technology to finance will require more than experience on Wall Street or a finance background. True innovators will also need a strong background in technology. In the case of Vocean, a team has been constructed that features leaders with both strong financial experience and deep roots in technology. The key person who is working on Vocean's blockchain platform has been working as a core member of Bloomberg's infrastructure team for over ten years. (And in my opinion, Bloomberg is the Google of Wall Street.) I wanted to spend so much time on Vocean in this chapter because I think it's the best example of what can be accomplished when more and more professionals from traditional industries contribute to blockchain innovations. The experience and expertise they bring will make astounding things possible and will help ensure that blockchain become appetizing to different industries.

THE FUTURE OF BLOCKCHAIN IN THE FINANCIAL INDUSTRY

It's important to remember that it took the Internet over twenty years to really ensconce itself into our daily lives. In the early 2000s, the Internet in China was still very slow, and you couldn't do much on it. Now, we simply can't live without it! We Chinese are on it almost all the time (except maybe when we're sleeping). Blockchain is experiencing the same adoption period. It was originally created as a tool to allow cryptocurrency to store transaction information. But now, if you look at Ethereum for example, there are over a thousand applications and functions available on it (in addition to storing cryptocurrency transactions).

The effectiveness of blockchain has enabled us to cut out intermediaries, too. For example, when banks issue a mortgage to an individual so that he or she can make a property purchase, those banks need to verify the ownership of the property and also check if the customer has applied for a mortgage before. These requirements introduce real estate brokers into the mix, and they play a major role in the selling and buying of the property. But with blockchain technology, every single piece of property will be documented into blocks of the chain. It will be transparent for everyone. People will be able to go to blockchain to check this information, instead of to a related third party. This will save time and eliminate costs.

Blockchain also has a bright future when it comes to Wall Street. According to Jerry Zhong, blockchain remains popular with many hedge funds, and that popularity is growing. But to become a viable option for replacing the centralized system of storing information (in the way Wall Street would like it to), blockchain needs to address two major issues—regulation and safety. The regulatory status of blockchain is still unclear, and the safety measures currently in place are still not adequate for many on Wall Street. Yet I believe these are solvable problems. And with Jerry Zhong at the helm, I think blockchain is going to lead us into the next industrial revolution.

5.

THE TOP OF THE FOOD CHAIN AND THE BIRTH OF CRYPTO EXCHANGES

L et's start this chapter with a simple question: what exactly is a crypto exchange?

Essentially, a crypto exchange is a digital marketplace in which traders can buy and sell cryptos using different fiat currencies (or other items of value). It's an online platform that acts as an intermediary between buyers and sellers. A crypto exchange functions similarly to a traditional stock exchange. It matches buyers and sellers, allowing customers to make trades.

The first such exchange was a Bitcoin exchange founded in October of 2009. It was named New Liberty Standard and was located in New York. It was a place where people could exchange Bitcoins for fiat money, or fiat money for Bitcoins. Martti Malmi, an early Bitcoin evangelist, supported New Liberty Standard by investing 5050 Bitcoins as seed money. In return, he received a whopping $5.02 USD via PayPal. When it was launched, New Liberty Standard estimated the value of Bitcoins based on the consumption of electricity per Bitcoin cost. Based on this valuation system, between October and November of 2009, the exchange rate between Bitcoins and US dollars was approximately 1000 to 1.

Back then, Bitcoin was the only cryptocurrency. Yet as more cryptocurrencies have been developed, crypto exchanges have had to evolve to support trading among multiple cryptos.

ERC-20 is a technical standard used for smart contracts on the Ethereum blockchain for implementing tokens. ERC stands for Ethereum Request for Comment. Today, ERC-20 drives an increasing amount of tokens into the crypto world through ICOs. ERC-20 was first proposed in November of 2015, and it functioned such that any token that complied with ERC-20 would be compatible with Ethereum wallets. With ERC-20, developers can also build apps (DAPPs), and people who build DAPPs usually issue tokens as "currency" to be used within the DAPP. These tokens are not allowed to be directly traded for fiat money. They have to first be exchanged for Bitcoin or Ethereum. However, the creation of ERC-20 is important to the history of exchanges because of the "currency within a currency" it makes possible. Clearly, the appetite for trading between cryptos is not diminishing.

Before China banned ICOs and crypto exchanges in late 2017, China-based exchanges were a major force in the global crypto market. BTCC, founded in 2011, is generally considered to have been the first crypto exchange in China. The volume of trading on BTCC was immense, among the top three global exchanges. Yet, like many others, BTCC was asked to close in 2017. Current exchanges like Huobi, OKcoin, and Binance were all founded by teams originating in China.

Exchanges are important because they're sort of "on the top of the food chain" of the crypto economy. They're also a place where true entrepreneurs and innovators rub elbows with speculators and scam artists. Their lack of regulation often creates a vacuum in which people can take advantage of one another. In the United States, Japan, and South Korea, all exchanges are registered domestically, which means that they exist under strict government regulation. China was one of the markets that initially adopted the strictest regulations for cryptocurrency. Yet China eventually decided the risk was not worth the reward and shut them down completely.

THE FIGHT BETWEEN CENTRALIZATION AND DECENTRALIZATION

The crypto exchanges that we have been talking about here have mostly been centralized exchanges.

Centralized exchange trading provides benefits like the facilitation of liquidity, the assurance of transparency, and the ability to pin trades to the current market price. It is true that there are certain risks associated with exchange trading—such as inner management risks, unethical business practices on the part of the exchange itself, and the potential for asset misappropriation fraud. However, decentralized exchanges can address many of these risks and issues. If you compare centralized exchanges with decentralized exchanges, you'll find big differences between the two.

Centralized exchanges provide services like Know Your Customer, custodian services, and asset clearance. Centralized exchanges also provide sophisticated solutions for clients in terms of asset management. They have flexible approaches when it comes to charging clients. These exchanges will charge users trading fees, initial listing fees related to ICOs, and so forth.

Decentralized exchanges, on the other hand, were once the hottest thing in the crypto market because of their different approach. In June of 2017, Bancor Protocol initiated a crowd-funding ICO to establish a multilayered system of currency wherein one token could be be "reserved" for another. It aimed to set the new standard for cryptocurrency exchanges. (As a decentralized exchange, Bancor Network relies on smart contracts to match trades and execute them automatically.) The ICO raised $153 million worth of Ethereum. (By then, the market price of Ethereum was $273.) It was the most valuable ICO in history at the time. Bancor's ICO also received the endorsement of well-known investors, including Tim Draper, the American venture capitalist. (Even though Bancor has a very successful ICO, it would not be correct to say it has become "the star" of decentralized exchanges. The twenty-four-hour trading volume of Bancor is only $6 million, far behind competitors like Kybernetwork and IDEX.)

Decentralized exchanges like Bancor's satisfy all the demands of investors and traders that centralized exchanges fail to address. Centralized exchanges use a strong ICO filtering system that many find too exclusive. Decentralized exchanges support the trading of any token based on ERC-20. Decentralized exchanges also have a lower market barrier than centralized ones. Some ICOs that are less fortunate in their "launch phases"—meaning they don't receive cornerstone investments or cannot afford the cost of being in centralized exchanges—find that decentralized exchanges remain an effective way for them to raise capital.

EtherDelta is an important cautionary tale in this space. It was one of the biggest and most dominant Ethereum decentralized exchanges. About 230 different tokens were actively traded on it. Many ICOs would use it to offer exclusive token sales to investors and institutional investors two days before they were available to the public. Because of this, EtherDelta was a popular starting point for ICOs and at its peak had millions of users.

Whenever a cryptocurrency gets more attention—and experiences a corresponding increase in market value—the exchanges carrying it draw increasing attention from hackers. Hackers try their best to find any loopholes in the exchanges that will allow them to steal cryptos. (We have talked about the DAO project that ultimately forced Ethereum into two blockchains.) Safety and security were also the issues that brought down EtherDelta. Many users trusted implicitly that a decentralized exchange would be safe from hacking. However, EtherDelta was hacked multiple times. EtherDelta doesn't use a traditional computer server. Instead, it's all backed up on Ethereum blockchain using a smart contract. It is a true DAPP, a distributed app existing in the crypto world. When users trade on EtherDelta, they need to create a wallet that can talk to the smart contract. EtherDelta is what's often called a "wholesome wallet solution." EtherDelta users need to input a public key and a private key when they access their wallets. It is this step that puts users in a spot where they become the target of hackers.

EtherDelta has been hacked three times. Until recently, hackers attacked by entering the safety loopholes in EtherDelta and inputting malicious code that would farm private keys from users' wallets and then steal their tokens. But in December of 2017, hackers directly targeted the exchange's DNS server, which shocked everyone and resulted in losses across the exchange. EtherDelta has now lost the trust of most of its users and is largely considered a "has-been."

THE FUTURE OF EXCHANGES: THE COEXISTENCE OF CENTRALIZATION AND DECENTRALIZATION

Centralized exchanges and decentralized exchanges are both going to be around for a long time. Centralized exchanges still dominate the market in terms of liquidity and traffic, but decentralized exchanges are sticking around.

Decentralized exchanges built upon Ethereum were once believed to have stronger defense systems, and many felt they could grow in popularity because of their resistance to hacking. However, as cases like EtherDelta proved, nothing is ever truly "unhackable."

The fundamental idea of cryptocurrency (as well as blockchain) is to decentralize, but for the moment, in terms of practical application, centralized exchanges have a stronger economic foundation and a more dominant place in the market.

Business-wise, centralized exchanges have a solid model. They charge users trading fees and charge token sale fees related to ICOs. Leading centralized exchanges are realizing profits in the millions on a daily basis, simply due to the overwhelming volume of the trading they facilitate. (According to Recode, Coinbase, an American Bitcoin exchange, had revenues of over $1 billion in 2017. Binance, now based in Japan, expects a net profit of $500 million to $1 billion in 2018, according to its chief executive officer, Changpeng Zhao. And the volume of cryptocurrency trading is only going to increase in the days ahead.)

Centralized exchanges have the added appeal of being able to cover users' stolen tokens. Decentralized exchanges are not able to do this. On June 19, 2018, one of the world's largest cryptocurrency exchanges, Bithumb, experienced one of the most severe hacking incidents in cryptocurrency history, resulting in losses of $30 million. In the aftermath, Bithumb promised to refund the hacking victims' losses using its own reserve.

Centralized exchanges are constantly spending to improve their security, and to take care of the messes left after a hack. Because the exchanges are so profitable, they have the resources to do this. And their doing so helps maintain the reputation of the entire industry.

Because of what they provide and how they work, centralized exchanges are becoming more and more similar to entities like NASDAQ and the New York Stock Exchange. Centralized exchanges have developed well-established trading systems that attract ICOs and investors. They are even beginning to attract "market makers." In the traditional financial industry, market makers can be brokerage houses or independent security dealers who assist investors with the selling and buying of securities. Market makers provide liquidity to the market and make it easy for investors to sell and buy at any moment. Decentralized exchanges support person-to-person trading, but their lack of market makers may become yet another hurdle.

SOME SECRETS OF EXCHANGES

The initial listing fee for an ICO on a centralized exchange can be a lot of money. How much exactly? Currently, there is no agreed-upon standard. The cost of listing an ICO on an exchange largely depends on the liquidity and structure of the exchange itself. Exchanges with high liquidity will charge more to list an ICO. The cost will also be related to the "heat" of the ICO. During the peak of the ICO market in 2017, the cost to list an ICO on a centralized exchange crept to between $1 million and $2 million on the top ten exchanges with the highest liquidity levels. Compare that to what stock exchanges charge for an IPO. According to NASDAQ, the initial listing fee of an IPO is usually between $125,000 and $300,000 (excluding the yearly listing fee). Yet for many startups and investors, an ICO is a much easier way to raise capital. Startups benefit from the low cost of money, and early investors like getting in on exciting young technologies before everyone else. Keeping ICOs attractive in the future will be the single factor that most determines if the success of these exchanges continues. Not all exchanges profit through their initial listing fees. Some have instead implemented community voting as part of the selection criteria for new tokens, and they charge a small fee for each vote. (This helps ensure that fake or fraudulent coins not be introduced and also gives the exchange a tidy profit.) Voters pay each time they cast a ballot. More votes means more support for an ICO, and more profit for the exchange.

Bibox, an exchange that I cofounded, uses both an initial listing fee and community voting to select and list ICOs. A few high-quality projects will be listed on the exchange directly after providing legal papers and paying an initial listing fee, but the rest go through the community voting procedure. To stay competitive in this fast-evolving industry, Bibox is constantly improving its community voting mechanism to make the process easier and better. In Bibox's earliest days, community voting was much more simple and direct. Any user could simply open an account on Bibox and start voting. Today, voters pay one token (issued by Bibox) each time they vote. One person can vote 10,000 times if he or she wants to.

Some exchanges have also introduced the "super node" model. To be a super node in the community, a person (or a group of people or institutions) must reserve a certain amount of tokens issued by the exchange. They are also required to have investments with the exchange. But the votes of these super nodes, as you might imagine, can settle an issue once and for all. Initially, super nodes were only seen in crypto investment funds. Now, however, the model has slowly been migrating into traditional venture capital spaces.

The notion of "consensus" is a concept that's bigger than crypto. It can touch all aspects of human society. But when it comes to the financial world, consensus can be dominated by institutional investors or powerful groups. This is a problem, because it's a reversion back to centralization. Community consensus ought to be a way to create balance between elites and the majority. That's why Bibox's next step will be to introduce third-party valuation into the consensus-reaching process. Under our model, one third of voting rights will be given to super nodes, one third will be the community's, and the rest will be reserved for the exchange itself.

Tokens issued by exchanges play a big role in determining community power. Whether it's a super node or an individual investor, voting is always going to be based on how many tokens a group or person holds. In the case of Bibox, each community member is entitled to voting rights equivalent to tokens held. Before voting for an ICO, each voting member needs to reserve a certain amount of tokens.

Let's look at MakerDAO. It's a company that aims to create a "decentralized stablecoin" cryptocurrency tied to the US dollar. Their coin is called DAI. It uses a smart contract-based managing system. In their community, the more users hold onto the coin, the more voting rights they will have when it comes to issuing more DAI next year. Ideally, under this model, everyone is supposed to be involved in the community voting process.

There are always new models popping up that we can learn from. Fcoin is another good example, having recently become one of the top ten global exchanges. Fcoin introduced the concept of "trading is mining" in June of 2018, and it has been attracting many investors and traders. This model came about after a loophole was exploited in Fcoin's way of doing business. Fcoin announced it would cease using 30 percent referral fees. The day after the announcement, its trading volume decreased by 5 percent. But with the launch of the "trading is mining" model, it has become more successful than it ever was before! The model of "trading is mining" is innovative and exciting, and others are adopting it. Coinpark, for example, has also moved to a "trading is mining" format. Yet Coinpark goes even further than Fcoin. Newly listed tokens go to Bibox first, and the ones who "survive" the filtering system will then go to Coinpark. It is essentially an exchange for quality tokens!

Who can say what innovation will come next?

The Future of Crypto Exchanges: External Regulation and Self-Regulation

The future of crypto exchanges probably depends a lot on the industry's appetite for self-discipline. As I noted at the outset, exchanges are commonly known as the "top of the food chain." They control the ebb and flow of trade and play a crucial role in the token economy. Exchanges are not supposed to support insider trading in either the prime market or the secondary market. Because of their influence, any policy or rule an exchange introduces will probably have a powerful influence on the market as a whole. In the early days of crypto, there were many "gray areas" when it came to crypto exchanges. Many investors made a fast buck with unethical business practices. Yet the crypto exchanges expelled the bad elements because they had to. There was no other way to continue to exist. It is my belief that to move forward effectively, the exchanges will have to acknowledge that their journey of self-improvement is far from over.

Due to increasing competition among exchanges, many seem tempted to shirk self-discipline and self-regulation. Accordingly, even in crypto-friendly countries, government regulation is becoming more intense. In January of 2018, the South Korea Blockchain Association attempted to thwart further regulation by launching a self-regulatory program. The Japanese Blockchain Association is working on something similar. It remains to be seen if these efforts will be enough.

Across the board, exchanges needs to increase their self-defense capabilities. Cryptocurrency is continually growing and evolving, and so must the security that protects it. With crypto marching headlong into the mainstream financial market, it would be a shame if it tripped and fell because of unaddressed security needs. According to CipherTrace, in the first two quarters of 2018, $731 million worth of cryptocurrencies were hacked, tripling the total figure for all of 2017. Phishing sites and DDos attacks are continuing to impact the reputations and accountability of exchanges of all sizes and types. Clearly, we are not yet doing enough. Addressing security capabilities will be absolutely critical for the long-term sustainability of the industry.

Cryptocurrency is traded between countries and across boundaries of every type. But even so, different countries have different regulations regarding these cryptos. Governments impose these kind of regulations out of fear, and out of a lack of understanding. To avoid a dark future without crypto, it is up to all of us to make the case that we are not opposed to any regulation. In fact, it must be shown that crypto *can* be regulated. The best case scenario, of course, is that the industry is able to show that it is trustworthy enough to regulate itself.

6.

THE SECONDARY MARKET: LOW-LYING LAND

In the previous chapters, we've covered basic elements of crypto economy—including cryptocurrency, smart contracts, distributed ledger-based DAPPs, ICOs, and tokens. We've also explored how crypto exchanges support direct trading between major cryptocurrencies and fiat money, as well as trading among and between different cryptocurrencies. And we've reviewed how ICOs have established themselves as a powerful new way of raising capital in crypto world.

Yet all of above is generally happening in what I like to call "the primary market." And when an ICO is listed in a crypto exchange, it also has to confront investors from the secondary market. The secondary market is kind of similar to the stock market. But because cryptocurrency is still young, when it comes to secondary market influence, we are seeing phenomena that can be quite unusual.

THE SECONDARY MARKET OF LOW LIQUIDITY

There is imbalance between the prime market and secondary market. That's the first thing to understand. The prime market has become standardized and has been so ever since traditional VC came onto the ICO evaluation scene. Many quality ICOs have been received well in the prime market. However, these same ICOs often get the cold shoulder when they're listed on the secondary market. There are many reasons for this.

Liquidity reveals how strong a project is in terms of potential cash-out. In a market where there are fewer buyers than sellers, sellers will lower their trading price to attract buyers. In the crypto world, this decreases the value of tokens. The twenty-four-hour trading cycle of the prime market is frenetic and crazy, but the secondary market remains extremely inactive. There are hundreds of tokens being traded in the secondary market, true, but investors do not see any liquidity.

The reason behind this mainly arises from people trying to make quick money in the secondary market. When ICOs reach the secondary market, the prices are much higher than they were in the prime market. Accordingly, shareholders of an ICO often try to cash out before the prices go down in the secondary market. However, prime market investors making fast money and cashing out leaves a mess for the individual investors in the secondary market who have purchased the tokens at the peak of their price. An ICO is like a stock that needs constant buying and selling to maintain its liquidity and value. When early investors in the ICO cash out their shares, it makes it very challenging to maintain stability.

When a blockchain startup launches an ICO, it's usually still in its early stages. Once it is listed in the market, the startup may find it is not able to keep up with innovations it promised to deliver on paper. What then makes such a situation even worse is when the shareholders try to cash out, which in turn drives the anxiety level of the whole market up. True, some strong projects do continuously improve their service and technology and see their quarterly net profits reliably increasing. However, we cannot assume that this will always, or even typically, be the case.

The design of the early token economy is certainly not perfect. In a traditional financial market, before a company launches an IPO, the CEO and management team design a thoughtful plan detailing how shares will be offered, and price of shares, in a way that ensures the liquidity of the stock after the IPO is launched. But many blockchain projects launch an ICO without sufficient experience (or any experience). This lack of experience usually reveals itself when the secondary market comes in to play. Currently, there are just not enough competent financial teams available to help startups to properly analyze all pertinent aspects of their offerings. As a consequence, many companies overoffer shares to investors when conducting the ICO launch. For example, many only reserve 10 percent of issued tokens, meaning 90 percent of tokens will go flooding into the market, which makes it possible for speculators to manipulate the prices. Once a bad actor controls over 50 pecent of the tokens of one ICO, the team on the project will have no control over the tokens or the prices of the tokens in the secondary market. This kind of situation happened a lot in the early days of the cryptocurrency market. Many investors took advantage of insider information to make a quick buck off of people in the secondary market. While the overall situation has improved, the lack of strong regulation still hurts liquidity in the secondary market (as well as some investors in the prime market). Yet, so far, the majority of ICOs are still using the utility token format. They are not traded in markets where security regulations are fully developed. The role the SEC is playing—or hints that it may play—is increasingly critical. Total transparency would greatly increase market liquidity. As it stands, the violent up and down of token values in the secondary market remains a major issue. (Just look at the market prices at which Bitcoins are valued in different countries.)

According to crypto expert Vincent Molinari, many ICO offers are still no more than schemes—a way for a few people to cash in. Yet he believes when regulation is in place, the market value will return to a reasonable level, these schemes will go away, and all good actors will benefit over time. Long-term investment will become the rule and not the exception. Consider that in the prime market of an ICO, it usually takes six months to a year to turn capital into profits. Whereas, in traditional VC, as I noted earlier, it usually takes ten years.

As we wait for regulation to be put into place (either from within or without), the token economy is nonetheless constantly evolving on its own. By learning from the past, new ICOs will improve by offering fewer shares so as to have better control of the project and the market prices of issued tokens. In this connection, many investment institutes are already playing important roles in stabilizing the secondary market and increasing confidence in investors.

The cryptocurrency trading provider Altonomy recently launched a crypto "index fund" that includes the top five digital asset trading funds—Bitcoin, Ether, Ripple, Bitcoin Cash, and Litecoin. As a digital asset management provider, Altonomy is aiming to help investors enhance their crypto returns. As the market continues to stabilize, we can probably expect to see more funds like this arrive on the scene.

THE UNREGULATED MARKET MAKER

During the process of launching a typical Wall Street IPO, companies often hire market makers to increase liquidity, and also to support the price of the stock. Market makers enable the smooth flow of financial markets. The SEC defines a "market maker" as any firm that stands ready to buy and sell stock on a regular and continuous basis at a publicly quoted price.

In cryptocurrency, most startups will hire market makers to increase the liquidity of their tokens in the first three months of the ICO. Since the end of 2017, there has been a flood of market makers coming into the ICO scene. This is because the secondary market for cryptocurrency is similar to the traditional financial market in terms of operation. Market makers coming into the cryptocurrency space serve the same purpose as when they're working in the traditional stock market. But because of the absence of regulation, market makers in the crypto secondary market are not required to be licensed. Some are still very professional and helpful. But, of course, some are not. Many market makers do little to help increase market liquidity and facilitate trades. Instead, they are only facilitating arbitrage. Accordingly, anyone working in this space should be very careful when dealing with them.

HOT MONEY IN THE SECONDARY MARKET

Due to the lack of regulation (and/or the lack of enforcement), cryptocurrency often finds its secondary market flooded with speculators and manipulators. Whether you're a quant or a non-quant, it's easy to see that there are many opportunities in cryptocurrency that do not exist in the traditional market. I personally know investors who have made a fortune in crypto using short-term quant strategies. There are several reasons why they've been able to do this.

First and foremost, many different stock exchanges exist in the secondary market. One token might be traded on multiple exchanges. The prices of one token might be very different from one exchange to another. Many traders invest and profit through the difference in price of the same token on different exchanges.

Second, in the futures market, both Okex and Bitmap support futures trading. This trading can be leveraged a hundredfold. Though the price difference can be very small, if the risk is manageable, the return can be huge. Many people have made fortunes this way.

And finally, the secondary market can be rigged by manipulators. If you put major currencies such as Bitcoin and Ethereum aside, many of the tokens you'll find issued through ICOs are there to be manipulated. These tokens are similar to penny stocks. And everyone wants to believe they've discovered the next Bitcoin and Ethereum.

The problems facing the secondary market in crypto are similar to the problems that were faced by American stock exchanges 100 years ago. When a market lacks certain regulations and oversights, predictable things happen. Pump and dumps are very common in the secondary market of cryptocurrency, just as they were on the US stock exchange so many years ago. Fraudsters spreading false news about new cryptos in a chat room have a great deal in common with con artists who sent false telegrams with information that might impact a stock in 1919.

In any traditional financial market, the practice of market manipulation is illegal. And it should be. The lack of regulation that lets some people make a quick dollar hurts everyone else because it hurts our faith in the system.

When contrasted with the traditional stock market, the cryptocurrency market will always have an innate uniqueness. This won't change even when it becomes more regulated. Stock markets are usually open between 9:30 a.m. to 4 p.m. on weekdays, meaning trades only happen during this specific time frame. It allows for high-volume trading and high liquidity, but you can't trade on weekends or at midnight. In contrast, the secondary market of cryptocurrency will always be open twenty-four hours a day.

OTC—Big Players

We've discusses the importance of liquidity and investor confidence in the secondary market. Now I'd like to discuss OTC (Over The Counter) trading, and its importance for the top 1 percent of investors and traders in cryptocurrency world.

OTC is a relatively simple concept. An OTC trade is done directly between two parties without the supervision or facilitation of an exchange, but buyers and sellers still need to find each other to close that trade. In the world of cryptocurrency, OTC is mostly used for fiat-to-cryptocurrencies trades. (Exchange trading is mostly comprised of trades among different tokens and cryptocurrencies.)

Why does OTC exist in the first place? Well, the financial market is a bit like a domino. When you push one down, it will trigger a chain reaction. In an exchange where information is transparent, a very large movement of cash will trigger sudden price movements in the market—which has the potential to impact the person or group of people behind the trade. Many would prefer to go the OTC route and keep things quiet.

OTC traders dealing in amounts over $250,000 are often called "whales." Other customers are often called "small fish." People on exchanges such as Huobi and Binance are often individual traders. This is the visible market that the majority of crypto players are most familiar with. But the liquidity of the visual market is restricted by the number of individuals participating at any moment. It's also restricted by which currencies carry which liquidity. Exchanges are like retail shops on the street, open to everyone. When a whale shows up in the market to purchase a large amount of cryptocurrencies, the whole market goes up. This is usually referred to as "slippage." For big players, OTC is the preferred option precisely because it's not supposed to generate a sudden market up or down. OTC traders can be private traders, brokers, or institutions. Their major function is to provide security during the buy to avoid turbulence on transparent exchanges. The crypto exchange Altonomy serves as an OTC provider and puts its own funds into the platform to secure the liquidity of OTC trades. Increasing liquidity means maintaining a relatively stable and reasonable price for buyers and sellers. Once the price is set, Altonomy will offset the risk in the market. Meanwhile, a price for the trade will be decided. For example, if a buyer is considering purchasing a certain amount of Ethereum, Altonomy will generate a relatively low price that will also have a low influence on the market.

Despite the secretive nature of specific trades, OTC trading has a profound influence over the cryptocurrency market. The liquidity of exchanges is only going to go up as more and more individuals come into the game. OTC also provides a strong support function exterior to the traditional exchanges. For example, the price of Bitcoin and Ethereum is largely dependent on its prices in OTC trading. The volume of OTC trading also reflects the market liquidity and market cap. OTC also influences the confidence of future cryptocurrency trades. The more trades made through OTC, the more confidence is injected into the market. If the amount of cash being invested into the market decreases, so will the confidence in cryptocurrency. According to an OTC trading desk (with whom, full disclosure, my company has a collaboration), the cash flowing into the crypto market in January of 2018 was only two-thirds of what it was in 2017. As a result, the whole market was suffering from poor liquidity, and fewer trades were made during this period.

Currently, in addition to Bitcoin, OTC trading can be found in traditional venture capital, family office trading, and hedge funds. But due to a lack of regulation, many pension funds, banks, and wealth management companies stay out of the market entirely. However, there's a major OTC desk called Circle, where you'll find very high-profile investors such as Goldman Sachs, DRW, Genesis, Smart Contract, and Octagon Strategy. According to Reuters, Circle's daily volume of digital assets trades was between $1.5 billion and $2 billion during December of 2017 alone. In addition, I should note that Skype and Google Voice are places where OTC trades can also take place.

THE FUTURE OF THE SECONDARY MARKET

Regulation is going to decide the future of the cryptocurrency secondary market. Money held by traditional financial institutions wants to come in. It's stopped by a lack of sufficient liquidity, yes. But it's also stopped by a lack of regulation.

Regulation by the SEC of things like custody services would help traditional investors decide to what degree digital assets may be safely invested into the market. According to Coinbase, about $200 million worth of digital assets are currently "watching the SEC" and waiting to be invested. Once an effective solution to custody services appears, all those digital assets will join the market, which will increase market liquidity wonderfully.

An SEC decision to regulate crypto trading products would also impact the influence of institutional investors. So far, the SEC and CFTC (Commodity Futures Trading Commission) have shown themselves to be very fond of derivatives. Yet limited tradable cryptocurrencies are not giving a lot of incentive for old money to come into the market. In July of 2018, a Chicago-based exchange handed in an application for a Bitcoin ETF to the SEC. Previously, Gemini and Winklevoss had tried to apply for an ETF with the SEC. (We'll have to wait and see if this one takes.) Having more financial derivatives available will increase liquidity in the secondary market. According to a Reuters report from March of 2018, the

British exchange house Coinfloor will soon begin selling Bitcoin futures. Their product targets hedge funds, sophisticated individual traders, and Bitcoin miners.

So far, US regulators haven't been interested in creating specific regulations for crypto exchanges. Accordingly, the crypto market lacks the sophisticated financial products needed to attract big players. This will be a barrier not just for the secondary market, but for the whole crypto industry in the days ahead.

7.

BEYOND BOUNDARIES— CRYPTO ECONOMICS AROUND THE WORLD

B y design, blockchain transcends individual nations and states. Perhaps for this reason, it is often associated with the idea of globalization. We know from even the most cursory glance at history that every major technological innovation makes the world smaller. The most recent culprit was the Internet, which made the world smaller by bringing people together in exciting new ways. I believe that the application of blockchain to finance will bring humans even closer to one another. It will also, in my opinion, unleash revolutionary positive changes onto society.

It is true that blockchain technology is still young. But despite this, we have already seen the powerful benefits it can bring into our lives. These include cross-border payment capability, early capital raising, and improvements to securities. The applications of blockchain and cryptocurrency are challenging the existing financial market. The attitudes about how quickly to adopt new technologies vary from country to country. So in this chapter, I'd like to shine a little light on blockchain innovations in different countries around the world.

SWITZERLAND—THE CAPITAL OF BITCOIN IN EUROPE

Switzerland has long been a haven for bankers, traders, and other financially minded people. Today, it is also emerging as *the* place for crypto innovation in Europe. People in finance have long known that Switzerland is an effective place to grow new businesses, because it pairs a stable infrastructure with financial expertise and resources. Finance is the main industry in Switzerland, and the Swiss have one of the highest average incomes of any country in Europe. According to the WEF 2015 report, Switzerland ranks at the very top when it comes to global economic competitiveness. These factors combine to make Switzerland one of the most attractive countries for blockchain and cryptocurrency developers.

Switzerland is famous for remaining neutral in times for war. Perhaps this temperament is also the reason why its government seems to be comfortable with supporting financial decentralization. The government of Switzerland has been actively involved in fostering the evolution of blockchain and cryptocurrency. Zug, a small city in Switzerland, has even embraced the nickname "Crypto Valley." Outsiders are generally aware of the extent to which Switzerland provides robust financial services to clients (and also respects their privacy), but it is fast gaining a reputation as a place where decentralized financial tools can grow. The probusiness environment, lack of regulation, and low tax rates in this country have attracted many entrepreneurs and high-end professionals. Perhaps it should be no surprise that Switzerland is now considered to be "the nest" for new innovations in blockchain. Ethereum's headquarters is located in Zug, and many lesser known cryptos are joining it there.

The government of Switzerland was also one of the first to accept cryptocurrency as payment. As one of the active early adopters of blockchain and cryptocurrency, Zug began allowing residents to pay for city services with cryptos back in 2016. But the city hasn't stopped there. They are also exploring the real-life application of blockchain in other areas, such as government. Voting in Zug was already possible via mail, the Internet, or at polling stations. But the city recently allowed residents to take part in a blockchain-based vote-casting test. The potential of broader use of blockchain is being realized here in a very real way.

Another major attraction for crypto entrepreneurs in Switzerland involves the launch of ICOs. Because the headquarters of Ethereum is in the country, the standard for an ICO is commonly accepted as ERC-20. Switzerland saw this opportunity and grasped it at the very earliest stages the industry. The results speak for themselves. So far, of the eleven biggest ICO launches of all time, four have taken place in Switzerland. In 2017, capital raised through ICOs in Switzerland surpassed $550 million USD and represented 14 percent of total ICO capital raised globally.

pwc   strategy&

Largest ICOs are hitting the USD 100mn mark – of which 4 out of 6 are hosted in Switzerland

The 15 biggest ICOs

		Total raised amount (USDmn)*	Status	End of ICO	Duration (days)	Industry	Focus	Country
1	Tezos	238.1	Past	14.07.2017	14	Technology	Smart contract platform	Switzerland
2	Filecoin	203.6	Past	07.09.2017	28	Technology	Data storage network	USA
3	EOS	159.2	Past	11.06.2018	5	Technology	IT Infrastructure	USA
4	Bancor	156.6	Past	12.06.2017	<1	Fintech	Cryptocurrency	Switzerland
5	The DAO	142.5	Past	27.05.2016	28	Fintech	Venture capital platform	Switzerland
6	Status	95.0	Past	20.06.2017	<1	Technology	Messaging platform	Switzerland
7	TenX	83.1	Past	24.06.2017	<1	Fintech	Digital-only bank	Singapore
8	Press.one	82.0	Past	19.07.2017	7	Technology	Content publishing	China
9	MobileGo	47.6	Past	24.05.2017	30	Entertainment	Gaming marketplace	USA
10	SONM	41.2	Past	19.06.2017	4	Technology	IT Infrastructure	Russia
11	Basic Attention Token	36.0	Past	31.05.2017	<1	Technology	Browser	USA
12	Stox	33.3	Past	16.08.2017	15	Fintech	Prediction market platform	Canada
13	Polybius	32.4	Past	06.07.2017	36	Fintech	Digital-only bank	Estonia
14	Civic	29.4	Past	22.06.2017	2	Technology	Security/ data storage	USA
15	Storj	25.4	Past	25.05.2017	6	Technology	Cloud storage	USA

Date: 11.09.2017

* Calculations based on currency exchange rates on end date of ICO. As Ether and Bitcoin exchange rates are highly volatile, actual and current market capitalization of the companies today may differ significantly from figures shown in the table. ICO funding amount until 11.09.2017 considered.

Source: PwC Strategy& analysis

Strategy& | PwC

So what about security? Money laundering has long been a major concern of Switzerland's private banking industry, and some worried that crypto could exacerbate this. In order to catch up with the increasing popularity of ICOs—while preserving security and preventing fraud—in early 2018, the national Financial Market Supervisory Authority (FINMA) clarified some key rules regarding regulating ICOs and tokens. According to the new rules, there can be only three types of tokens, and each token is limited to its own function. The goal of this clarification is to help investors make wise decisions and prevent the intentional dissemination of confusing information.

When we look to the future, we see Switzerland's banking and financial industries actively involved in the development of digital assets and blockchain. Falcon recently became the first Swiss private bank to provide blockchain asset management solutions to its clients. Its services enable the bank to exchange and hold Bitcoins for traders using their cash holdings. And to dive even deeper into the world of digital assets and blockchain, Falcon has also entered into a collaboration with the Swiss brokerage firm Bitcoin Suisse to add Ether (ETH), Litecoin (LTC), and Bitcoin cash (BCH) to its blockchain asset management offerings.

To attract more startups, Crypto Valley has been setting up the infrastructure needed for the world of digital assets and blockchain services. In 2017, the Crypto Valley Association was founded (with sixteen founding members, including PwC, Thomson Reuters, and iProtus). Under the leadership of Oliver Bussman, the former CIO

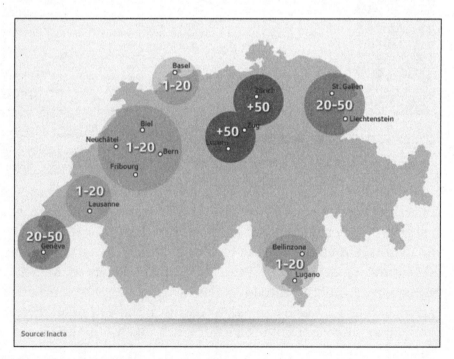

Source: Inacta

of UBS, the Crypto Valley Association aims to further develop Crypto Valley into the world's best and most nurturing ecosystem for crypto technologies and businesses.

Through this open-minded approach, Switzerland has positioned itself as the leader in cryptocurrency and blockchain technology in Europe. In 2018, at a crypto finance conference for private and institutional investors, Swiss Economics Minister Johann Schneider-Amman went even further and said that Switzerland wants to be the "crypto nation." It is a positive signal, at a national level, that the government has confidence in the future of crypto. This attitude will definitely attract more and more blockchain and crypto startups to the country.

CHINA: CRYPTO IN EXILE

As we all know, China is one of the countries regulating cryptocurrency most strictly. However, it is also one of the most active markets for cryptocurrency. Of the ten leading crypto exchange houses, three originated in China. China was once the top market for cryptocurrency, a fact that encouraged the rapid development of these Chinese crypto exchange houses. But since the advent of strict overregulation, the game has been utterly changed.

Huobi was started in September of 2013 as an exchange supporting direct cryptocurrency and fiat money. Huobi grew rapidly and at one point was the largest digital assets exchange platform in the world. OKcoin was also founded in 2013. Alongside Huobi, it is the Chinese exchange platform known for dominating the cryptocurrency trading market in China. Between 2013 and 2017, all Chinese exchange platforms supported fiat money and cryptocurrency direct exchanges, which made the process of getting into crypto simple and easy.

In 2017, Binance was launched as a new platform for crypto-to-crypto trading. The founder was the CIO of OKcoin. Unlike Huobi and OKcoin, Binance only supported exchanges among different cryptocurrencies. As a relatively new player, Binance's server was not located in mainland China, and the business was licensed overseas. This gave Binance the flexibility to avoid certain regulations.

Then it happened.

On September 4th, 2017, the People's Bank of China declared that all initial coin offerings (ICOs) were illegal and ordered that all tokens sales should cease immediately. Then, on September 19th, the government of China ordered all Bitcoin exchanges to close within the month. The government-mandated ordered shutdown rattled crypto markets all over the globe. One by one, exchanges closed. Both Huobi and OKcoin decided to leave China in order to survive elsewhere. They worked with Chinese regulators to do this in a legal manner and started transferring the services to overseas providers like Huobi Pro and Okex.

There are opportunities in every crisis. The shuttering of cryptocurrency exchanges in China provided a great opportunity for Binance, since it was not licensed in China. All Chinese trading has largely moved to Binance since the ban.

Another window that opened as the door was closed in China was in ICO and secondary markets. The year 2017 is considered to be the best year for ICOs globally. According to Coindesk, there were 43 ICOs launched in 2015, but there were 343 in 2017. Token sales and the trading of small cryptocurrencies—as opposed to major ones such as Bitcoin—have become increasingly popular among Chinese investors. As I noted in the previous chapter, in sharp contrast to major cryptocurrencies, small cryptocurrencies are relatively easy to manipulate. Small individual investors flooded into the secondary market, hungry for these currencies. After Huobi and OKcoin were shut down, Binance stepped in to fill the void. Within half a year, Binance became the largest exchange in China.

China was once the most active market for Bitcoin and investors in cryptocurrency. However, when the government's iron hand forced major exchanges to leave, it changed everything. Globally, the price of Bitcoin dropped from about $4,300 to about $3,300. But by the end of 2017, the price of Bitcoin had bounced back to

Summary Stats

	Close Date 年				
	2014年	2015年	2016年	2017年	2018年
ICO Size ($mn)	30	9	256	5,482	8,117
Average	4	1	6	16	24
Median	2	1	1	8	14
Max	18	5	152	262	850
Min	0	0	0	0	0
Std. Dev.	7	2	23	28	70
Number of ICOs	7	7	43	343	334

almost $20,000 before falling again. To me, this just further proves that cryptocurrency is capable of decentralization. It will evolve when it needs to. The survival ability of cryptocurrency—and the whole set of industries surrounding it—is just remarkable. And it is only getting stronger. Opportunities are continuing to grow.

THE ASIAN MARKET—PROSPERITY FOR THE CRYPTO INDUSTRY

Asia, as a continent, has become a major player in the crypto industry. Among countries in Asia, Japan and South Korea are currently on top. China has made her negative attitude very clear, but Japan and South Korea have articulated a preference in the opposite direction.

Japan is now considered the most crypto-friendly country in Asia. According to coinhill.com, the Japanese yen accounts for 56.2 percent of Bitcoin (BTC), the most popular cryptocurrency. The yen is followed by the US dollar at 28.4 percent. (The Chinese yuan accounted for the largest share until January of 2017, but the government restrictions made short work of that.) In Japan, cryptocurrency is still very popular as an investment. This is thanks in large part to the positive attitude that the Japanese government maintains toward it.

In April of 2017, Japan revised its Payment Services Act to legally define "virtual currency" as a form of payment. (Japan still does not define Bitcoin as legal tender, but it acknowledges that you can use it to legally purchase things.) In July of 2017, Japan also ended an 8 percent consumption tax on Bitcoin, which further encouraged the trading of cryptocurrency in that country. Over 200,000 business owners in Japan now accept Bitcoin as payment. In Tokyo, Bitcoin is now accepted at all locations of Bic Camera, the nation's electronics retailing giant.

The Japanese government is still closely watching over cryptocurrency exchanges, and there *is* some regulation. Exchanges now have to verify customer identification for major transfers as a safeguard against money laundering and terrorism. Harsher standards have also been put in place for exchanges that disobey the law. Exchanges also have to register with the FSA (the Financial Services Agency of Japan). The agency has inspectors visit the exchanges regularly to examine their operations and verify the number of employees. The FSA has granted licenses to sixteen cryptocurrency exchanges so far.

Despite safeguards, Japanese exchanges have still found themselves the victims of hacking incidents, some of them quite severe. In response, the FSA says it is building a defense system to protect investors and other players involved in cryptocurrency. The Japan-based Mt.Gox exchange was once the busiest exchange in the world, handling 70 percent of all of the Bitcoin transactions. Then, in 2014, it was the victim of the most famous and massive hack of all time when 850,000 thousand Bitcoins were stolen, a crime that impacted 750,000 different users. At the time, the Bitcoins were valued at around $450M. In early 2018, the second-largest exchange in Japan, Coincheck, also lost NEM tokens valued at $534 million to a hack.

Despite some devastating setbacks, Japan is still the most supportive Asian country when it comes to encouraging cryptocurrency innovation. After tackling security at currency exchanges, the Japanese government is next moving to tackle the ICO market. In April of 2018, the Center for Rule-Making Strategies at Tama University released a list of guidelines for regulating ICOs. This government-backed report strongly suggests that ICO projects shall clearly present how all funds will be distributed at the outset of the ICO. The template also includes new rules for tracking the progress of an ICO, for confirming the identity of buyers, and for eliminating insider trading. The Japanese public generally seems to see these guideline as a friendly signal to ICOs. Japan is trying to bring ICOs into the mainstream financial system through sophisticated supervision and careful regulation. It's an excellent approach.

South Korea is another active market for virtual currency. The South Korean virtual currency market started growing exponentially in March of 2017 and peaked in June that same year. South Korea has a population of only 51 million people but has the highest per capita crypto-ownership rate of any country. Less than 1 percent of Americans own virtual currency, but over 30 percent of South Koreans do.

In South Korea, institutional investors are not allowed to participate in the virtual currency market. Because of this, most investors in virtual currency are simply private individuals. There are a couple of reasons why crypto is so hot in South Korea. One is that South Korea is among the most advanced digital economies in the world, and among the most technologically advanced. Digital currency has found its natural habitat in South Korea. Because of their enthusiasm for all things high tech, investing in cryptocurrency is second nature for South Koreans. The other reason for this popularity is probably the high yield that can be realized through investing in cryptocurrency. The success of Ethereum, for example, has been a big story in the South Korean media.

In contrast to Japan, South Korea has not issued many clear regulations to guide cryptocurrency trading. Its rate of tax on crypto assets is also not very clear.

However, to increase transparency in the trading process (and to help prevent money laundering), South Korea did adopt a "real-name" crypto trading policy on January 23, 2018. This policy forbids anonymous, untraceable transactions. Instead of using virtual accounts, users have to trade through bank accounts to verify their identities. So far, six banks have stepped up to offer virtual currency accounts. And to avoid being left out, the top four crypto exchanges have moved to real-name accounts. (These include Bithumb, Upbit, Coinone, and Korbit.) Not everybody likes the "real-name rule," and many see it as something hampering the growth of the crypto market in South Korea. For many investors, the requirement makes it too difficult to transfer fiat money into virtual currency market accounts.

Like China, South Korea also banned ICOs. In September of 2017, the Financial Services Commission (FSC) in South Korea announced that all initial coin offerings would be banned. The FSC claimed it was taking this step because the trading of virtual currencies needed to be more tightly controlled and monitored. It was not more specific.

Compared to the Chinese exchanges forced into exile, the crypto exchanges in Japan and South Korea are relatively safe under government regulation.

OTHER PLACES WHERE CRYPTO IS GROWING RAPIDLY

Heading back to Europe, I want to note that Malta has also become a very attractive country for crypto exchanges. Binance recently announced its intention to move to Malta, and Okex is about to open an office in Malta, too. On July 4th, 2018, Malta approved three regulatory bills designed to encourage crypto adoption. The bills are the Malta Digital Innovation Authority Act, the Innovative Technological Arrangement and Services Act, and the Virtual Financial Asset Act. These new laws are designed to provide clear regulation for companies using blockchain technologies in a way that will encourage innovation. It's a move designed to lure crypto companies and blockchain startups to the island—and it's working. Malta's low tax rate probably doesn't hurt, either.

Singapore is a similar case to Malta. Since China and South Korea banned ICOs, Singapore has positioned itself as an Asian alternative for companies exploring ICOs. For many years,

Singapore has been a major global financial center. But it is now also a very blockchain-friendly country. And in addition to ICOs, Singapore has emerged as a harbor for blockchain startups. The government is encouraging companies to come there to innovate in blockchain technology. Distinguishing it further from Malta, Singapore also has a very well-established financial infrastructure. This combination of friendly attitude, open-minded spirit, and physical infrastructure makes Singapore *the* place for Asian companies to do ICOs now.

Tax havens have long been attracting attention from companies that raised capital through ICOs. Since the US and China do not allow ICOs, many companies that would like to do Initial Coin Offerings have accordingly set their sights offshore. Through the use of Variable Interest Entities (VIEs), most British Virgin Island (BVI) ICOs are now structured through an ICO issuer incorporated as a BVI business company, which is possible under the BVI Business Companies Act of 2004 (the BCA). There is no specific regulation of any kind on ICOs in BVI. So, as you might imagine, it is poised to emerge as another hotspot.

Cryptocurrency was born out of the ideology of decentralization. One of its goals is to encourage people to participate in transactions without third-party overseers. Despite these lofty ambitions, virtual currency has also had to learn to play along with the regulations local governments around the globe have seen fit to impose. The bear market of 2018 indicates the consequences of a lack of regulation. Large amounts of money are waiting for more regulation before they enter the crypto market. As it stands, traditional financial institutions have insufficient confidence in cryptocurrency and the crypto trading system. This limits the future possibilities for crypto economics. We want to enjoy freedom, but not create chaos. A balance must be struck. Exchanges that provide crypto trading platforms are rapidly globalizing. With more and more countries introducing clear, sensible regulation, I believe that crypto exchanges will survive and thrive, especially those that can bring themselves to play along with the government.

8.

GETTING ALONG WITH REGULATORS

If 2017 is remembered as the Year of the ICO, then I think history will look back on 2018 as the Year of ICO Regulation. The cryptocurrency market cap has been rising since the beginning of 2017. The steadily increasing number of ICOs is forcing regulators to take second and third looks at the regulation of the crypto market. Many entities in the US are now actively involved in formulating suitable regulations for the crypto economy.

ICO SCHEMES : CRACKING DOWN ON BAD EGGS

After a year of soaring Bitcoin prices, people everywhere began to realize the money-making potential in this market. About 30,000 cryptocurrency-related domain names were registered in 2017 around the peak of Bitcoin's price. Many of these domains, however, appeared to be tied to scams or tricks. In addition to fake addresses, false marketing materials, and promises of over 4 percent daily interest, some of these unsavory sites even used unauthorized photos of high-profile individuals and celebrities to entice investors. Lack of regulation gives speculators a chance to take advantage of ICOs and of the less-regulated crypto market as a whole.

Austin, Texas, is one of the technology centers in the United States, and the State of Texas was one of the first to bring the hammer down on these ICO schemes. In May of 2018, the Texas State Securities Board (TSSB) shut down the cryptocurrency promoters

Bitcoin Trading & Cloud Mining and Forex EA&Bitcoin Investment LLC.

Forex EA&Bitcoin had fraudulently offered tenfold profits on an investment within twenty-one days. Bitcoin Trading & Cloud Mining LTD had claimed that it owned three Bitcoin mining farms and proposed to offer investors 4.1 percent daily interest on mining Bitcoins.

On May 16, 2018, the TSSB shut down another ICO in Houston. This one was called Wind Wide Coin. The company's website displayed fake endorsements from Jennifer Aniston, Prince Charles, and former Finnish Prime Minister Matti Vanhanen to deceive investors. Not only was this business using unauthorized photos of celebrities, Wind Wide Coin was not even registered as a business with the government.

Joe Rotunda, director of enforcement at the TSSB, told CNN in an emailed statement that the con at Wind Wide Coin was "strikingly familiar" to others that the state had shut down in recent months:

> Today's action is a reminder that, step by step and case by case, we've been uncovering a virtual playbook of tactics employed by promoters of illegal and fraudulent cryptocurrency investment programs. Although their names may change and their products may vary, these promoters are employing surprisingly similar schemes. They are often promising lucrative returns from sophisticated investments tied to cryptocurrencies, and then manipulating photographs, media, testimonials and other online information to deceive the public into believing their claims.

In February of 2018, New Jersey issued a ban against token sales from Power Mining Pool (PMP), a European-based cryptocurrency business. It has also been permanently banned from conducting business in North Carolina. In Alabama, state government came down on the crypto mining companies LEV, Platinum, and Extabit and banned them from making sales. Colorado's state government investigated two ICO companies based in the state, and Massachusetts has permanently banned five ICOs.

Many crypto scams operate similarly to multilevel marketing or Ponzi schemes. But sometimes, even experienced investors may find it hard to keep up with the scammers and their tricks. As the ICO market grows, more scammers are trying their best to deceive investors. The problem is real, and it is serious. According to Coindesk, the Federal Trade Commission believes that American consumers lost $532 million to cryptocurrency-related scams in the first two months of 2018. That's staggering. Furthermore, that number could potentially grow to $3 billion by the end of 2018. Investors may lack knowledge and education regarding the crypto market, but a lack of swift action from enforcement agencies doesn't improve the situation (and only encourages the criminals).

The trick with ICOs is that different institutions hold different attitudes. In the last chapter, we reviewed what enforcement agencies in different countries around the world have decided to do. In the United States, the jury is still out. Regulators are playing it conservative. They are holding back. They haven't said "No" but they haven't said "Yes," either.

ATTITUDES ABOUT BLOCKCHAIN

In the United States, the federal government has not exercised its constitutional preemptive power to regulate blockchain. Instead, it has decided to leave the issue to state governments. According to Business Insider, in June of 2015, the State of New York became the first state to regulate cryptocurrency. By 2017, at least eight more states had laws on the books.

According to *A Comprehensive Overview of 50 States' Guidance and Regulations on Blockchain and Digital Currency*, Arizona is one of the most forward-thinking states when it comes to embracing the adoption of blockchain. The Arizona state government has passed several rulings that are actually in favor of blockchain. For example, HB 2417 makes signatures, electronic transactions, and contracts on blockchain legally valid. And SB 1091, a bill still under consideration, would allow residents to pay tax in cryptocurrencies such as Bitcoin.

In contrast to Arizona, New York has emerged as the state with the most negative attitude toward blockchain. The New York Department of Financial Service (NYDFS) established a regulatory framework that any virtual currency businesses is required to abide by—the famous BitLicense (or 23 NYCRR 200). This is a license that every company or individual is required to obtain if they plan to do crypto-related business in New York. As if this weren't enough, the process of getting the license takes a long time, and many who apply are not accepted. So far, New York has only offered the license to Circle, Ripple, Coinbase, bitFlyer, Genesis, and Xapo—that's six companies total. Investment banks such as Goldman Sachs who are considering diving into the cryptocurrency market would be required to obtain the BitLicense, as well.

Regulation needs to keep up with technology, not hinder it. Will there be a perfect balance between keeping consumers protected and allowing technology to grow? Perhaps not, but we have to keep trying.

THE LEGALIZATION OF CRYPTOCURRENCY: A LONG WAY TO GO

The excitement brought about by Bitcoin's rise and fall over the past couple of years has finally put it on the radar of the Internal Revenue Service. If you look at the IRS's virtual currency guidance posted on its website, you'll get a real sense of this entity's attitude about crypto. It isn't pretty. Virtual currency transactions are taxable by law just like financial transactions involving anything else, but back in November of 2016, the IRS asked Coinbase, one of the largest crypto exchanges, to hand over the financial data of 13,000 customers. Early in 2018, Coinbase finally complied with a court order and fulfilled the IRS request. The stated purpose of the request was to seek out those who were intentionally evading cryptocurrency taxes. However, I think it was also the IRS sending a signal that they were through pussyfooting around.

The Commodity Futures Trading Commission (CFTC) and the Securities and Exchange Commission (SEC) are also major forces in the regulation of virtual currencies. Most cryptocurrencies have qualities and traits that ought to make them fall under the regulatory provenance of the SEC. But according to Federal Reserve Chairman Jerome Powell, the cryptocurrency market is not yet big enough to pose a threat, and the US central bank is not looking to regulate it. The Fed, it should be noted, does not have jurisdiction over cryptocurrencies. Federal agencies such as the SEC already oversee many crypto-related businesses, products, and trades. The CFTC has categorized Bitcoin and similar virtual currencies as a commodity. This has led many to believe that the CFTC ultimately has a favorable and sympathetic attitude regarding cryptos. Moreover, Gary Gensler, chair of the CFTC, has stated, "there's really nothing behind gold either . . . what's behind it is a cultural norm. For thousands of years we liked gold. We use it as a store of value, so Bitcoin is a modern form of digital gold. It's a social construct."

Meanwhile, the SEC is applying securities laws to everything from cryptocurrency exchanges to the digital asset storage companies known as wallets. The regulatory position of the SEC is not to ban every single ICO, but to regulate them and make them better serve investors (as well as the financial industry as a whole).

In the course of writing this book, I interviewed the Winklevoss Twins. Among their accomplishments is the founding of Gemini—a crypto exchange under the regulation of the US government. The famous brothers are also among the early investors in Bitcoin, a move that made them billionaires. I'd like to use their words to close this chapter:

> We believe strongly in thoughtful regulation and the many benefits it brings for all market participants. The US financial markets are some of the healthiest and most vibrant

markets in the world because they have regulatory oversight and rules in place. As a result, Gemini is a New York trust company regulated by the New York State Department of Financial Services (NYDFS), which we believe makes it the most regulated digital asset exchange and custodian in the world.

This is not intended as legal advice, but US regulators, namely the CFTC, have determined that Bitcoin is a commodity, similar to gold. As a result, Bitcoin is what many call a virtual commodity, and similar laws that apply to gold in the US apply to Bitcoin. ICOs that are securities need to register with the SEC and follow securities laws like any other non-cryptocurrency security in the United States. The US has over 80 years of laws and regulations in place for securities, so issuer requirements are well understood for those issuing ICOs that qualify as securities under the Howe Test.

9.

BLOCKCHAIN—ASSETS PROTECTOR

The rapid development of blockchain and the crypto economy has attracted a lot of attention from hackers. We've reviewed some prominent examples. ICO token sales are usually the "sweet spot" for hackers. As I mentioned, the DAO is a great example of this. Exchanges themselves are now targeted by hackers. Suffice to say, security is going to be absolutely critical to the next stage of token economy. In this chapter, we will discuss the security solutions that will be required to address these issues.

Both private blockchains and public blockchains have security issues. Private blockchains give their operators control over who has access to the information stored in the chains. Public blockchains, in contrast, are open to everyone. Because of their prevalence and dominance, I will mostly be focusing on the security issues related to public blockchains.

A tremendous amount of effort has already been devoted to making protections stronger and defending assets on blockchain. I'd like to begin by looking at two approaches.

CERTIK: MATHEMATICAL VERIFICATION SOLUTIONS TO SECURITY ISSUES

Blockchain was designed to be unhackable. However, the involvement of smart contracts has created some openings through which bad actors can sometimes enter and cause trouble. Bitcoin and Ethereum are supported on public blockchains, which have a higher defensive ability, but when it comes to smart contracts, the shorter, less complex codes involved can make them more hackable. The upshot is, of course, that smart contracts become the #1 target for hackers.

Compared with traditional software security, blockchain security suffers from three main limitations:

Primarily, in most cases, the coding of a smart contract is open-source, which means that all the DAPPs coding sources are available to the public. Everyone can see who created the codes. Accordingly, a hacker can try to take advantage of this public information.

The irreversibility of the smart contract is another limit. This quality makes it harder to take care of a mess after the fact because the smart contract will always execute terms. It is very hard to change the terms in a smart contract once it has been released into blockchain. It is also incredibly expensive to do.

The final limitation comes from the fact that many vulnerabilities and loopholes are driven by "rookie mistakes." Not all DAPPs feature state-of-the-art design. With any DAPP, you may find mistakes after it is already up and running. And since the smart contract is not reversible, the original design of a DAPP has to be seamless, which is almost impossible to accomplish. For example, users of Cashierest, a South Korean crypto exchange, found out that they could withdraw up to five times the amount they'd requested from the exchange. This bug was caused by an internal system error affecting withdrawals. Foxbit, a Brazilian exchange, also experienced a notable bug. Users found that they could change their two-factor authentication settings using only one password, which made it easier for hackers to lock genuine users out of their accounts. There was no email confirmation, no security question, no other security protection. And in the end, it was very easy for hackers to withdraw the users' funds.

Certik is a formal verification platform for smart contracts and blockchain systems. It wants to improve security by providing smart contracts and blockchain ecosystems that are bug-free and hacker-resistant. Since it is almost impossible to correct mistakes once a smart contract has been put into execution, it is critical to make sure the design of the smart contract is perfect. Certik has developed a "layer-based approach" that takes the prohibitive large proofing and quality-check tasks and turns them into smaller ones.

The cofounder of Certik, Zhong Shao, earned his PhD in computer science from Princeton University and is the Thomas L. Kemper Professor and department chair in the department of computer science at Yale University. For the past twenty years, he has devoted himself to highly visible research in the fields of cybersecurity, programming languages, operating systems, and certified software. He and his group at Yale have also developed the world's first hacker-resistant concurrent operating system, CertiKOS, which can build cyber-physical systems that are probably free from software vulnerabilities.

So it's clear that while major issues still exist, we've got some of the smartest people in the world working vigorously to solve them. Let's look at another example.

SENTINEL PROTOCOL: BLOCKCHAIN TO PROTECT BLOCKCHAIN

Sentinel Protocol is a company that provides solutions to blockchain security issues. It is often described as a security intelligence platform for blockchain (SIPB).

We know that a decentralized cryptocurrency system can, on the one hand, give users the freedom to do transactions across national boundaries and without interference from intermediaries. But on the other hand, as we've seen, its lack of an adequate defense system often poses a threat to users and their assets. If you deposit your cash with Chase and it's somehow stolen from your account, the bank will take care of it. Chase will use its centralized system to trace the money and get it back for you. (And if they somehow fail to do this, you could go to the police and report the theft.) But in the decentralized world, it would be a different scenario because of the nature of anonymity. Sentinel Protocol is attempting to step in to fill that security vacuum.

Patrick Kim is the founder of Sentinel Protocol. In 2016, 7,218 Ethereum were stolen from his virtual wallet. He informed the operator, who was luckily able to resolve the issue. However, the incident motivated Kim to dig deeper into the world of blockchain security, user experience, and individual user protection.

Blockchain is overwhelmingly safe. Remarkable security has now been achieved for Bitcoin and Ethereum. The remaining security problems at this point mostly lie within applications, with DAPP, and with individual end users. Consumers need new, adaptable methods to solve their remaining security problems. This is the mission of Sentinel Protocol. According to their latest white paper, Sentinel is now developing three products intended to address the most pressing security issues remaining for the decentralized world. The products are Threat Reputation Database (TRDB), S-Wallet, and D-Sandbox.

TRDB operates by collecting threat data from many different sources, including cryptocurrency exchanges, virtual wallets, payment services, and even IT and security companies. It is a little like a Wikipedia for collectable threat data. For example, such information can be the wallet address of hackers, a Malicious URL, phishing websites, or anything similar. TRDB is only updated by authorized experts, which allows it to maintain the highest levels of precision. However, regular users can also participate in the data collecting process by allowing automatic reporting, as well as submitting information manually. In addition, TRDB is constantly honed through consultations with experts in information security.

TRDB is basically designed to solve two safety-related issues. One concerns the central server. Since everything is stored in one location under a central server format, it's easy to hack and easy to manipulate and abuse. The Internet is designed to have "User to Server" or " Server to User" functions. TRBD seeks to avoid hacks and keeps server information flowing smoothly and safely.

The other issue it addresses is the lack of communication among security providers and Internet security software companies. The more information on a threat that's collected, the less chance it has of resulting in a cybercrime. But since every Internet security company keeps its security data to itself, the benefits of building a shared database are not realized. TRDB allows this sharing safely and efficiently.

S-Wallet is a self-defense wallet. It keeps users safe by filtering transactions against wallet addresses with a history of scams. It also filters out Malicious URLs, URIs, and Malware. Just as TRDB collects information regarding threats, S-Wallet collects information allowing users to defend themselves against potential risk.

Distributed Malware Sandboxing, also known as D-Sandbox, is another important and innovative safety mechanism. It independently tests for suspicious and unidentified files or links by running virtual machines (VM) on decentralized nodes. This enhances security, prevents hacks, and closes potential ways in for cybercriminals.

The current lack of regulation requires ICO investors to do the homework themselves when it comes to security. There are still ways that blockchain-related investments can be vulnerable to cyber-crime. Yet dedicated investors who are truly passionate about cryptocurrency and blockchain will find ways to ensure that safety and security keep up with the rapid pace of innovation in this industry. Hacking, Internet fraud, and phishing can infect an ICO at almost any stage. For example, some hackers might build a phishing website that looks exactly like the real ICO website in order to fool potential investors. Because of tactics like this, protective measures will always be necessary. Sentinel Protocol is providing powerful and meaningful solutions in this area. In the near future, Sentinel Protocol hopes to work with exchanges to assist governments in detecting criminal money laundering. (Their product known as Anti-Coin-Solution, or ACM, is specifically designed for this task.)

Certik and Sentinel Protocol are great examples of the constant, ongoing efforts that are required to effectively resolve security issues in blockchain and cryptocurrency—and, at the same time, to build a new blockchain ecosystem with the highest levels of security. Forging this new, safer future will require experts in computer science, data analysis, and decentralized ledger technology. The decentralized world is still at a sort of "starting point." Though some very talented people are already on the job, we need to ensure that this world be appealing to the next generation of security experts. But I don't think that will be a difficult sale to make. Truly, blockchain is where all the opportunities are.

10.

THE FUTURE OF
BLOCKCHAIN

There's a quote I love from Bill Gates. It goes like this: "We always overestimate the change that will occur in the next two years and underestimate the change that will occur in the next ten. Don't let yourself be lulled into inaction."

I like this so much because it says something about human nature. People are quick to forget all that happened over the previous ten years, which leads them to underestimate the potential change that will come in the next decade thanks to new technology. In previous chapters, we've looked at the remarkable changes that blockchain technology has made possible. In the years to come, I believe a whole new financial ecosystem built and centered around blockchain and cryptocurrency will become the norm. This brand-new system will exist detached from the dominant fiat money systems that will still be in place but will have regulation under the government closer to that of fiat money. It will pose a challenge to the regulators as governments are forced to make adjustments to adapt to this new, other financial ecosystem. The crypto economy currently stands at around $300 billion. Though it still can't compare to the fiat money-based economies of the world, it's still enormous and undeniable. In this last chapter, I'm going to let my imagination run wild a little bit and explore the potential innovations that I think could make crypto and blockchain explode even more dramatically in the years to come.

WILL CRYPTOCURRENCY EVER BE ACCEPTED ON MAIN STREET USA?

Cryptocurrency starts off with this ideology of radical decentralization and degovernmentalization and gradually finds its way from small group of cypherpunks to the general public at large. But is that really so strange? How often do daring trends start as the fixation of a small group of evangelists but eventually find their way into everyone's lives in one form or another?

The relationship between cryptocurrency and the governments of the world is going to be the key element in the future of the crypto economy. I generally agree with an article I read on Investors.com earlier this year that laid out four possible future scenarios for cryptocurrency:

1. Global central banks will issue their own digital currencies. The Federal Reserve could issue its own digital currency, as well.
2. Large companies such as Amazon, Walmart, and Starbucks will issue their own digital coins as a way to establish trust and loyalty with customers, and to provide better service.
3. Retail giants will begin accepting crypto and in doing so will elevate Bitcoin, Ethereum, or another cryptocurrency above all others. The winner of this contest will offer safety, soundness, and utility.
4. Trust will be lost in government-backed fiat currencies, and a cryptocurrency future will come about by default. There may be a special likelihood of this in places like Venezuela, but it could also happen in countries like the US, where federal deficits are spiraling.

Yet these are only four perspectives, and there are others. Centralized institutions have a way of always wanting to regulate the decentralized world.

Crime has been associated with Bitcoin since the day it was born. Due to the convenience and anonymity it adds to transactions,

Bitcoin has been one of the easiest way for criminals to undertake illegal financial activities. Illegal transactions and trading have generated considerable amount of wealth for certain individuals. One well-known example is the Silk Road that was a Dark Web website that sold everything from drugs to stolen goods to Mafia "hits." It was designed to allow users to browse anonymously and securely with no potential for monitoring. Bitcoin was the chief currency used on the Silk Road. The FBI initially seized 26,000 Bitcoins from accounts associated with the Silk Road, worth approximately $3.6 million at the time. The site was ultimately shut down, and the mastermind behind it was sentenced to life in prison.

Though the Silk Road fiasco happened in the early days of Bitcoin, the cryptocurrency is still associated in the public's mind with money laundering and other illegal activities. As I've noted, different countries have different attitudes toward cryptocurrency and related financial tools. China and South Korea have banned ICOs, yet in some Mediterranean counties like Malta, cryptocurrency receives a warm welcome. The USA is still on the fence. The CFTC and the SEC—as well as individual states—have imposed some regulations on cryptocurrency and shut down some bad actors. For technology enthusiasts, the concern is that governments will shut down crypto *everywhere* if it is being used for illegal activity *anywhere*. For now, as the rapid growth of cryptocurrency continues, the shutting down of crypto entirely remains a very remote possibility.

Bitcoin and Ether have been acknowledged as commodities by CFTC, and Bitcoin futures have been accepted on the Chicago Mercantile Exchange (CME) and the Chicago Board of Exchange (CBOE). As to the true "value" of Bitcoin, we can reasonably compare it to gold. (To be clear, I'm not encouraging you to invest in Bitcoins here.) But two of the early investors in Bitcoin, who went on to become billionaires, the Winklevosses, have said they consider Bitcoin like a kind of "Gold 2.0." A place to store value. Personally, I think Bitcoin has the potential to hold stronger value than gold. The value of gold comes from its scarcity and durability.

But Bitcoin equals or surpasses gold when it comes to scarcity, portability, visibility, and fungibility. Bitcoin's portability is an additional benefit over gold. So far, Bitcoin has about a $300 billion market cap, while gold is at $6 trillion. The Winklevosses believe that Bitcoin could very well increase in value another twenty times over what it's worth today. In an interview with me, Tyler Winklevoss said he believes that one day the market cap of Bitcoin will equal or surpass that of gold. Still, there are uncertainties concerning Bitcoin as a store of value. The biggest among these may simply be the fact that there are still issues surrounding all cryptocurrencies. But the future will reveal itself as time goes by. We will have to be patient.

THE FINAL SCENARIO—THE BLOCKCHAINING OF ALL INDUSTRY

Rome wasn't built in a day. It will take time for blockchain to fully settle into our lives. But my closing thought here is that it's going to happen, and the impact will be enormous, widespread, and carry the potential to impact virtually all industries.

According to a report by Gartner, the business value-add of blockchain is projected to grow to slightly over $176 billion by 2025. It will exceed $3.1 trillion by 2030. Gartner also believes that the entire blockchain industry is still in its "irrational exuberance stage" in which the current applications of blockchain are actually not disruptive enough. In the days ahead, IT leaders will cut through the hype and move to apply blockchain across industries in order to realize the maximum possible benefit.

The world of the future will probably feature a combination of centralization and decentralization. Decentralized digital currency will be regulated and will have learned to "play along" with regulators in order to grow its ultimate financial potential. Creative applications of blockchain to other purposes will come very soon thereafter. Currently, the major innovations brought about by blockchain are still infrastructure-based. In the future, this will change. The speed and efficiency of blockchain will be increased across the board. And as the various public blockchains keep evolving, we will see more and more DAPPS specific to various industries. Those DAPPs will focus on disruptive innovation in blockchain applications, which will have enormous consequences for big data, cloud computing, AI, and more.

A recent CBIN Sights Report identified forty-two industries that stand to be heavily disrupted by blockchain technology. Finance is on the top of that list, including subsets like banking, hedge funds, and insurance providers. But other industries will be impacted, as well. These include real estate, healthcare, supply and logistics, and public affairs. Because blockchain is like an unlimited account book when it comes to documenting data chronologically, the data stored in blockchain are always open to everyone to see and check. This kind of transparent technology can be applied to industries that rely on data and collaboration. Just think of the possibilities!

So, will blockchain ever change the world in the way its creators intended it to? That might not quite be possible in today's climate. But as blockchain and cryptocurrency are further applied to the financial world, we will see decentralized exchanges and centralized exchanges working together. There will be a balance in the future. Blockchain is a technology that can bring us closer together, but it is still, like any technology, only as good as the humans behind it. As governments, regulators, and industries begin adopting and incorporating blockchain more and more, the interests of different communities will be both enhanced and protected. No matter what the founders' intentions were, this will be a satisfying outcome.

GLOSSARY OF TERMS

A

Altcoins

Altcoin is an abbreviation of "Bitcoin alternative." Currently, the majority of altcoins are forks of Bitcoin with usually minor changes to the Proof of Work (PoW) algorithm of the Bitcoin blockchain. The most prominent altcoin is Litecoin. Litecoin introduces changes to the original Bitcoin protocol such as decreased block generation time, increased maximum number of coins, and different hashing algorithm.

ASIC

An "Application Specific Integrated Circuit" is a silicon chip specifically designed to do a single task. In the case of Bitcoin, it is designed to process SHA-256 hashing problems to mine new Bitcoins. ASICs are considered to be much more efficient than conventional hardware (CPUs, GPUs). Using a regular computer for Bitcoin mining is seen as unprofitable and only results in higher electricity bills.

B

Bitcoin

A cryptocurrency that (1) runs on a global peer-to-peer network, (2) is decentralized (no single entity can control it), (3) is open-source (wallet & transaction verification), (4) bypasses middlemen or central authority, (5) with no issuer or acquirer, and (6) that anyone with a computer or smartphone can use.

Bitcoin ATM

A cash point where people can trade fiat currency and Bitcoins.

Blockchain

Shared, trusted, public ledger of transactions, which everyone can inspect but which no single user controls. It is a cryptographed, secure, tamper-resistant distributed database. It solves a complex mathematical problem to exist. A blockchain is a perfect place to store value, identities, agreements, property rights, credentials, etc. Once you put something like a Bitcoin into it, it will stay there forever. It is decentralized, disintermediated, cheap, and censorship-resistant. Applications of Blockchain: Bitcoin (cryptocurrency), Namecoin (wants to replace the entire DNS system of the Internet), Sia (a decentralized cloud storage), and Ethereum (Turing complete Virtual Machine, where you can run any smart contract). Any centralized service like eBay or Dropbox can potentially be built in a decentralized way using blockchain technology, considerably lowering transaction costs.

Block Explorer

A tool to see detailed information of transactions, accounts, and other activity on blockchain. Depending on the cryptocurrency, sweeping data or limited data are available.

Block Halving

Bitcoin's supply of new coins issued to miners is cut in half about every four years to keep it scarce. This 50 percent cut is known as halving. The next halving will be around 2020.

Block Height

Refers to the total number of blocks on a given cryptocurrency blockchain. It starts with the first block, also known as the Genesis Block (Height 0), and counts up from there.

Block Reward

Payment made to the volunteers who offer their computers to facilitate transactions on a blockchain network. The payment can be a mix of new coins and transaction fees.

Block Size

Shows the file size of each block on a blockchain and therefore how many transactions can be bundled and processed in each one. For Bitcoin, the current block size is 1MB.

C

Chain Linking

Chain linking is the process of connecting two blockchains with each other, thus allowing transactions between the chains to take place. This will allow blockchains like Bitcoin to communicate with other sidechains, allowing the exchange of assets between them.

Client

A software program a user executes on a desktop, laptop, or mobile device to launch an application.

Cloud Mining

Classical cryptocurrency mining requires huge investments in hardware and electricity. Cloud mining companies aim to make mining accessible to everybody. People just can log in to a website and invest money in the company that already has mining datacenters. The money is managed by the company, and it is invested in mining equipment. Investors get a share of the revenue. The disadvantage for the user is that cloud mining has low returns compared to traditional mining.

Consensus

A fundamental problem in distributed computing is to achieve overall system reliability in the presence of a number of faulty processes. This often requires processes to agree on some data value that is needed during computation. The consensus problem requires agreement among a number of processes for a single data value. Some of the processes may fail or be unreliable in other ways, so consensus protocols must be fault-tolerant. The processes must somehow put forth their candidate values, communicate with one another, and agree on a single consensus value. The Bitcoin blockchain uses electricity to ensure the security of the system. It creates an economic system where you can only participate by incurring costs and Proof of Work (PoW).

Consortium Blockchains

A consortium blockchain is a blockchain where the consensus process is controlled by a preselected set of nodes.

Cryptographic Hash Function

The cryptographic hash function is a mathematical algorithm that takes a particular input, which can be any kind of digital data, be it a password or a jpeg file, and that produces a single fixed-length output.

Cryptojacking

Cryptojacking is the secret use of a device to mine cryptocurrency. The first widely-known attempt at cryptojacking was the torrent tracker Piratebay. It enabled an in-browser mining software, so when somebody visits the website, his/her computer will start mining cryptocurrency via the browser. Users started noticing the unusual behavior in their browsers, and Piratebay took down the software. There have been many attempts at cryptojacking since then. The easiest way to find out if a computer is mining cryptocurrency is to check the resources monitor for unusual CPU behavior or to use the debug console of your browser and look for mining scripts. Developers also released Chrome browser extensions to protect users from mining occurring on their devices.

D

DAPP (Decentralized Application)

For an application to be considered a DAPP, or decentralized application, it must meet the following criteria: (1) Application must be completely open-source, and it must operate autonomously and with no entity controlling the majority of its tokens. The application may adapt its protocol in response to proposed improvements and market feedback, but all changes must be decided by consensus of its users; (2) Application data and records of operation must be cryptographically stored in a public, decentralized blockchain in order to avoid any central points of failure; (3) The application must use a cryptographic token (Bitcoin or a token native to its system), which is necessary for access to the application, and any contribution of value from miners/farmers should be rewarded with the application's tokens; and (4) The application must generate tokens according to a standard cryptographic algorithm acting as a proof of the value nodes are contributing to the application (Bitcoin uses the Proof of Work algorithm).

DASH

A type of cryptocurrency based on Bitcoin software but has anonymity features that makes it impossible to trace transactions to an individual and other capabilities. It was created by Evan Duffield in 2014 and was previously known as XCoin (XCO) and Darkcoin. For more information, visit the official website for DASH.

Decentralized

A state where there is no central control, power, or function or, in reference to infrastructure, no central point of failure.

Distributed Consensus
Collective agreement by various computers in a network that allows it to work in a decentralized, P2P manner without the need of central authority to deter dishonest network participants.

E

Ethereum
Ethereum is an open software platform based on blockchain technology that enables developers to write smart contracts and build and deploy decentralized applications (DAPPs). The native token of blockchain is called Ether, which is used to pay for transaction fees, miner rewards and other services on the network. The main innovation of Ethereum is the Ethereum Virtual Machine (EVM), which runs on the Ethereum network and enables anyone to run any application. The EVM makes the process of developing blockchain applications much easier. Before the emergence of Ethereum, developers had to develop a dedicated blockchain for each application they wanted to create. This process is time-consuming and resource-intensive. Ethereum will enable the development of many applications on the same platform, making the process much easier and more accessible for developers. The Ethereum Project, based in Switzerland, raised millions in seed money by premining and selling ethers to supporters and investors. As opposed to Bitcoin, its scripting language is Turing complete and full-featured, expandT ing the kinds of smart contracts that it can support. The Ethereum project wants to "decentralize the web" by introducing four components as part of its roadmap: static content publication, dynamic messages, trustless transactions, and an integrated user-interface.

F

Fiat
A term used to describe traditional government-issued and backed currencies like dollars, Euros, and yen. Not backed by physical commodities, but by legal tender laws.

Flippening

A potential future event, hoped for by Ethereum fans, where the total market cap of Ethereum surpasses the total market cap of Bitcoin—making Ethereum the most valuable.

FOMO

Internet culture term that stands for Fear of Missing Out. Describes actions taken by investors based on emotions and the fear of not benefiting from a price rise or drop.

Fork

A change to the software and rules of a cryptocurrency that creates two separate versions of the currency's blockchain. Forks can be softforks or hardforks; see below.

FUD

Internet culture term that stands for Fear, Uncertainty, and Doubt. It means negative information that is being purposefully spread about an asset to make people sell.

Futures

Contracts to buy assets (like cryptocurrencies and stocks) with an agreement for future delivery on a regulated stock exchange. Used to speculate on the future price of an asset.

G

Genesis Block

The very first Block in the blockchain.

H

Hardfork

A hardfork is a change to the blockchain protocol that makes previously invalid blocks/transactions valid and therefore requires all users to upgrade their clients. The most recent example of a hardfork in public blockchains is the Ethereum hardfork, which happened on July 21st, 2016. The hardfork changed the Ethereum protocol; therefore, a second blockchain emerged (Ethereum Classic, ETC) that supports the old Ethereum protocol. In order to continue existing, ETC needs miners, which would validate the transactions on the blockchain.

Hashcash
A Proof of Work system used to limit email spam and denial-of-service attacks that more recently has become known for its use in Bitcoin (and other cryptocurrencies) as part of the mining algorithm. Hashcash was proposed in May 1997 by Adam Back.

Halving
A reduction in the block reward given to cryptocurrencyy miners once a certain number of blocks have been mined. The Bitcoin block mining reward halves every 210,000 blocks.

I

Initial Coin Offering (ICO)
An unregulated means by which a cryptocurrency venture, typically early stage, can raise money from supporters by issuing tokens. It is often referred to as a "crowdsale," as ICO participants may potentially earn a return on their investments (as opposed to crowdfunding, where supporters donate money to a project or cause). Ethereum is currently the most popular platform for launching ICOs.

IOTA (MIOTA)
Refers to the cryptocurrency and the name of an open-source distributed ledger founded in 2015 that does not use blockchain (it uses a new distributed ledger called the Tangle). It offers features such as zero fees, scalability, and fast and secure transactions.

J

K

L

Light Node

A computer on a blockchain network that only verifies a limited number of transactions relevant to its dealings, making use of the simplified payment verification (SPV) mode.

Lightning Network

The Lightning network is a decentralized network using smart contract functionality on the blockchain to enable instant payments across a network of participants. The Lightning network will allow Bitcoin transactions to happen instantly, without worrying about block confirmation times. It will allow millions of transactions in a few seconds, at low costs, even between different blockchains, as long as both chains use the same cryptographic hash function. The Lightning network will allow two participants on the network to create a ledger entry, conduct a number of transactions between themselves, and, after the process has finished, record the state of the transactions on the blockchain. As for now, the Bitcoin network is capable of processing up to seven transactions per second. The Visa payment network, for instance, is believed to complete 45,000 transactions per second during a regular holiday period. This protocol tries to solve the Bitcoin scalability problem.

M

Mining

is the act of validating blockchain transactions. The necessity of validation warrants an incentive for the miners, usually in the form of coins. In this cryptocurrency boom, mining can be a lucrative business when done properly. By choosing the most efficient and suitable hardware and mining target, mining can produce a stable form of passive income. Multisignature addresses provide an added layer of security by requiring more than one key to authorize a transaction.

N

Node
Any computer that connects to the blockchain network is called a node. Nodes that fully enforce all of the rules of blockchain (i.e., Bitcoin) are called full nodes. Most nodes on the network are lightweight nodes instead of full nodes, but full nodes form the backbone of the network.

O

Off-Ledger Currency
A digital currency that is created (minted) outside of the blockchain ledger but used on the blockchain ledger. Example: government currencies that get used on the blockchain.

Offline Storage
Cryptocurrency wallets can be stored on devices and systems that are connected to the Internet or not. Offline storage is the latter case, providing additional protection from hacking.

On-Ledger Currency
A digital currency that is both created (minted) on the blockchain ledger and also used on the blockchain ledger. Most cryptocurrencies (like Bitcoin) are on-ledger currencies.

Online Storage
Cryptocurrency wallets can be stored on devices and systems that are connected to the Internet or not. Online storage is the former case, offering more convenience but also increased risk.

Open-Source

Collaborative and open software development approach that encourages experimentation and sharing. Project computer code is offered to others to work with and modify.

Oracle

For blockchain, an oracle is an automated system that decides based on preset rules and real-world events. It's an essential function that helps to arbitrate smart contracts.

P

Private Blockchains

A fully private blockchain is a blockchain where write permissions are kept centralized to one organization. Read permissions may be public or restricted to an arbitrary extent. Likely applications include database management, auditing, etc., internal to a single company, and so public readability may not be necessary at all in many cases, though in other cases, public auditability is desired.

Private Key

Each time a user runs a cryptocurrency wallet for the first time, a public-private key pair gets generated. The private key is a randomly generated number that allows users to transact over the blockchain. It is locally stored and kept secret. Each time a Bitcoin gets sent, a private key has to sign the transaction. This action is automatically executed by the wallet software. When a wallet asks users to do a backup, what this means is that the users must secure their private key. There are different types of wallets such as online wallets, mobile wallets, desktop wallets, hardware wallets, or paper wallets. The category of each wallet is determined by where private keys are stored. Online wallets are mostly provided by exchanges and keep users' private keys on their servers. If the service provider goes offline, users would lose access to their funds. Hardware wallets, for example, store users' private keys in a secure device that looks like a USB flash drive.

Proof of Authority(PoA)

A Proof of authority is a consensus mechanism in a private blockchain that essentially gives one client (or a specific number of clients) with one particular private key the right to make all of the blocks in the blockchain.

Proof of Stake

Proof of Stake (PoS) is a method by which a cryptocurrency blockchain network aims to achieve distributed consensus. While the Proof of Work (PoW) method asks users to repeatedly run hashing algorithms or other client puzzles to validate electronic transactions, Proof of Stake asks users to prove ownership of a certain amount of currency (their "stake" in the currency). Peercoin was the first cryptocurrency to launch using Proof of Stake.

Public Blockchains

A public blockchain is a blockchain that anyone in the world can read, to which anyone in the world can send transactions and expect to see them included if they are valid, and of which anyone in the world can participate in the consensus process—the process for determining which blocks get added to the chain and what the current state is. As a substitute for centralized or quasi-centralized trust, public blockchains are secured by crypto economics—the combination of economic incentives and cryptographic verification using mechanisms such as Proof of Work or Proof of Stake, following a general principle that the degree to which someone can have an influence in the consensus process is proportional to the quantity of economic resources that they can bring to bear. These blockchains are generally considered to be "fully decentralized."

Q

R

Ring Signature

Ring signature is a cryptographic technology that could provide a decent level of anonymization on a blockchain. Ring signatures make sure individual transaction outputs on blockchain can't be traced. A message signed with a ring signature is endorsed by someone in a particular group of people. One of the security properties of a ring signature is that it should be computationally infeasible to determine which of the group members' keys was used to produce the signature.

S

Satoshi

The smallest unit of Bitcoin, equal to 0.00000001 BTC.

Satoshi Nakamoto

A person or group of people who created the Bitcoin protocol and reference software, Bitcoin Core (formerly known as Bitcoin-Qt). In 2008, Nakamoto published a paper on The Cryptography Mailing List at metzdowd.com describing the Bitcoin digital currency. In 2009, it released the first Bitcoin software that launched the network and the first units of the Bitcoin cryptocurrency, called Bitcoins.

SHA (Secure Hash Algorithm)

A family of cryptographic hash functions published by the National Institute of Standards and Technology (NIST) as a US Federal Information Processing Standard (FIPS). SHA256 is an algorithm used in Bitcoin that takes an input of any size that can be any form of data (text, jpeg, pdf, etc.), mixes it up, and creates a fixed size output (a hash), which is 256-bit (32-byte) long.

Smart Contracts

Computer protocols that facilitate, verify, or enforce the negotiation or performance of a contract, or that obviate the need for a contractual clause. Smart contracts usually also have a user interface and often emulate the logic of contractual clauses. Proponents of smart contracts claim that many kinds of contractual clauses may thus be made partially or fully self-executing, self-enforcing, or both. Smart contracts aim to provide security superior to traditional contract law and to reduce other transaction costs associated with contracting.

Sidechains

Blockchains that are interoperable with one another and with Bit-coin, avoiding liquidity shortages, market fluctuations, fragmenta-tion, security breaches, and outright fraud associated with alterna-tive cryptocurrencies.

Softfork

A softfork is a change to the Bitcoin protocol wherein only previ-ously valid blocks/transactions are made invalid. Since old nodes will recognize the new blocks as valid, a softfork is backward-com-patible. This kind of fork requires only a majority of the miners upgrading to enforce the new rules.

Solidity

Solidity is a programming language designed for developing smart contracts. Its syntax is similar to that of JavaScript, and it is intended to compile into bytecode for the Ethereum Virtual Machine (EVM).

SPV (Simplified Payment Verification) Client

SPV clients are Bitcoin lightweight clients who do not download and store the whole blockchain locally. These wallets provide a way to verify payments without having to download the complete blockchain. An SPV client only downloads the block headers by connecting to a full node.

State Channel

State channels are interactions that get conducted off the blockchain without significantly increasing the risk of any participant. Moving these interactions off of the chain without requiring any additional trust can lead to significant improvements in cost and speed. State channels work by locking part of the blockchain state so that a specific set of participants must completely agree with one another to update it.

Swarm

Swarm is a distributed storage platform and content distribution service, a native base layer service of the Ethereum web three stack. The primary objective of Swarm is to provide a decentralized and redundant store of Ethereum's public record, in particular, to store and distribute DAPP code and data as well as blockchain data.

T

Token

In the context of Blockchains, a token is a digital identity for something that can be owned. Historically, tokens started as meta-information encoded in simple Bitcoin transactions, thereby taking advantage of the Bitcoin blockchain's strong immutability. At a protocol layer, tokens were outsourced extensions to Bitcoin's core protocol. Instead of being integrated as a feature on a software level, those tokens were created by misappropriating data fields in Bitcoin transactions (such as encoding data in the amount or op_return field). Today, modern tokens are created as sophisticated smart contract systems with complex permission systems and interaction paths attached. Smart contracts can be understood as software agents, which act deterministically and autonomously, within the scope of a given network, according to a predefined rule set. If the governance rules around issuance and management of a token are sufficiently complex regarding how they coordinate a group of stakeholders, token smart contracts may be understood as organizations sui generis. The management rules may reflect those of known legal, organizational entities such as stock corporations, but they do not have to.

Testnet
A test blockchain used by developers to prevent expending assets on the main chain.

Transaction Block
A collection of transactions gathered into a block that can then be hashed and added to the blockchain.

Transaction Fee
All cryptocurrency transactions involve a small transaction fee. These transaction fees add up to account for the block reward that a miner receives when he successfully processes a block.

Turing Complete
Turing complete refers to the ability of a machine to perform calculations that any other programmable computer is capable of. An example of this is the Ethereum Virtual Machine (EVM).

U

V

W

Wallet
A file that contains a collection of private keys and communicates with the corresponding blockchain. Wallets contain keys, not coins. Wallets require backups for security reasons.

Whisper

Whisper is a part of the Ethereum P2P protocol suite that allows for messaging between users via the same network that the blockchain runs on. The main task of Whisper will be the provision of a communication protocol between DAPP.

Whitelist

A list of registered and approved participants that are given exclusive access to contribute to an ICO or a presale.

Whitepaper

An informational document that generally informs readers on the philosophy, objectives, and technology of a project or initiative. Whitepapers are often provided before the launch of a new coin or token.

X

Y

Z